PLYMOUTH
THROUGH TIME
Derek Tait

AMBERLEY PUBLISHING

Acknowledgments

Photograph credits: The Derek Tait Picture Collection, Maurice Dart, Steve Johnson, Marshall Ware and Jerry Richards.

Thanks to all the people who have written to me over the years sending their memories and photographs.

Thanks also to Tina Cole, Ellen Tait, Alan Tait and Tilly Barker.

I have tried to track down the copyright owners of all photographs used and apologise to anyone who hasn't been mentioned.

Check out my website at www.derektait.co.uk

Bibliography

Books:

Images of England : Plymouth by Derek Tait (Tempus 2003).
Plymouth at War by Derek Tait (Tempus 2006).
Saltash Passage by Derek Tait (Driftwood Coast 2007).
St Budeaux by Derek Tait (Driftwood Coast 2007).
Plymouth Hoe by Derek Tait (Driftwood Coast 2008).
Memories of St Budeaux by Derek Tait (Driftwood Coast 2009).

Websites:

Brian Moseley's Plymouth Data website at: www.plymouthdata.info
Derek Tait's Plymouth Local History Blog at: http://plymouthlocalhistory.blogspot.com/

Newspapers

The Evening Herald
The Western Independent
The Western Morning News
The Western Weekly Mercury

First published 2010

Amberley Publishing Plc
Cirencester Road, Chalford,
Stroud, Gloucestershire, GL6 8PE

www.amberley-books.com

Copyright © Derek Tait, 2010

The right of Derek Tait to be identified as the Author of this work has been asserted in accordance with the Copyrights, Designs and Patents Act 1988.

ISBN 978 1 4456 0079 6

British Library Cataloguing in Publication Data.
A catalogue record for this book is available from the British Library.

Typeset in 9.5pt on 12pt Celeste.
Typesetting by Amberley Publishing.
Printed in the UK.

Introduction

Plymouth is an ever-changing city and new buildings alter the skyline constantly. The look of the city has changed greatly even over the last few years with drastic developments to the city centre including the building of the Drake Circus Mall. It's an unusual building that you either love or hate, which has not only changed the look of the city centre, but has also added a very odd backdrop to the bombed remains of Charles Church on Charles Cross Roundabout, which stands as a memorial to Plymouth's civilan war dead.

During the War, Plymouth was devastated by enemy bombing and much of the old city was lost forever. A new plan was put forward to construct a modern city with wide, modern streets and the heart of this still stands in the City Centre today. Many photographs within this book show the utter devastation which affected the city during the Blitz.

In this book, I have tried to show some of the great changes that have taken place in Plymouth over the years. The cityscape has vastly changed with the demolishing and rebuilding after the War and some scenes are almost unrecognisable today. As well as buildings, many modes of transport have also disappeared including trams and horses and carts. Even cars have changed dramatically over the years.

Amazingly, some areas have changed very little and the only difference appears to be modern lampposts, telephone masts, modern vehicles and wheelie bins. Some scenes have changed so much though that it's almost impossible to work out the location of the original photograph. The clues are there though and with a bit of detective work, including visits to the library and trawling through old newspapers, it soon becomes apparent where the original photograph was taken.

Some photographs included in this book aren't of exact locations but show the area where the activity in the first photograph took place as well as more of the wider picture to show the original location as best as possible. I think this makes it easier to work out where the photograph was taken originally and lets the reader see the changes and also to see if anything in the original photograph still exists.

A few photographs within the book feature old trams and many people might not realise what an extensive system of trams once ran through the city running from Derry's Clock in the City Centre, covering many parts of Devonport and Stonehouse and running as far as Saltash Passage, where passengers would get off to enjoy the annual Regatta, the Little Ash Tea Gardens, the St Budeaux Carnival or to continue their journey by ferry over the Tamar to Saltash.

Many train stations such as the ones at Millbay and Devonport have also long since disappeared. Millbay was once a very busy and popular station and many celebrities including Charlie Chaplin, Noel Coward, Harry Houdini and Laurel and Hardy would have passed through there. Chaplin and Coward were visitors of the Astors who lived at Elliot Terrace on the Hoe and Houdini and Laurel and Hardy appeared at the once popular Palace Theatre of Varieties in Union Street.

The book includes many photographs of the heart of the city but also features photographs of the Barbican, the Hoe and outlying districts. As well as transport, fashion has changed greatly and the whole city has become a vastly busier and more populated place.

I hope that you will find this collection of old and new photographs, together with their captions, both informative and enjoyable.

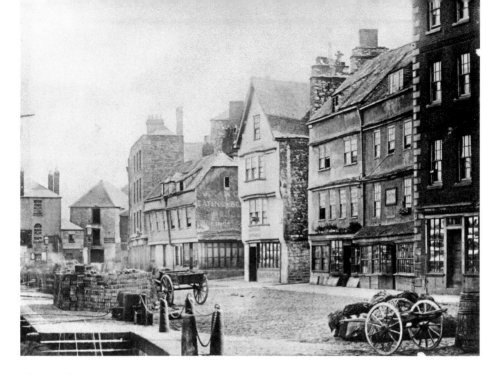

The Barbican

It's amazing how empty the scene is in the top photograph taken well over 100 years ago. At the time, there would have been much activity with fishermen offloading their catch. Some of the buildings have now been demolished but many remain. To the left of the bottom photograph now stands the Edinburgh Wool Mill which was originally the site of the old fish market.

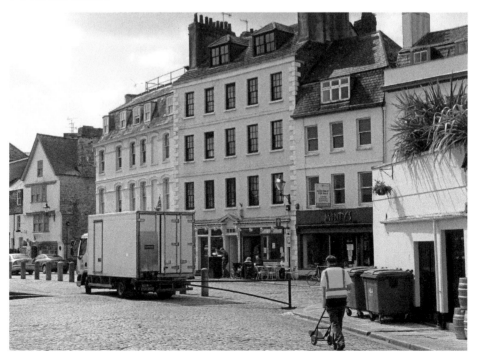

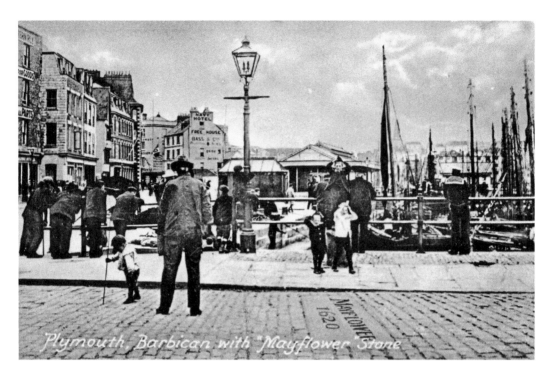

The Mayflower Stone, The Barbican

The fish market can be seen more clearly in the centre of the old photograph. Several Victorian children pose for the camera with their hands on their heads. On the right, a sailor gazes at the many fishing boats within the Quay. Many buildings seen in this photograph still remain although the modern picture shows several new buildings particularly the Mayflower Visitor Centre on the left.

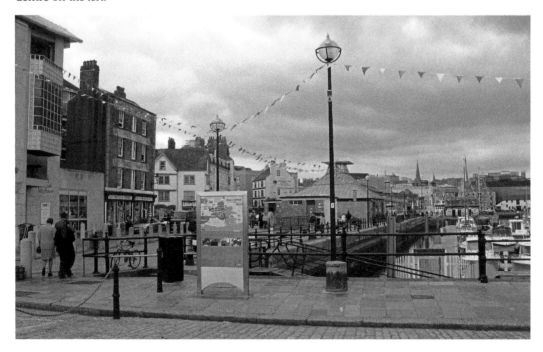

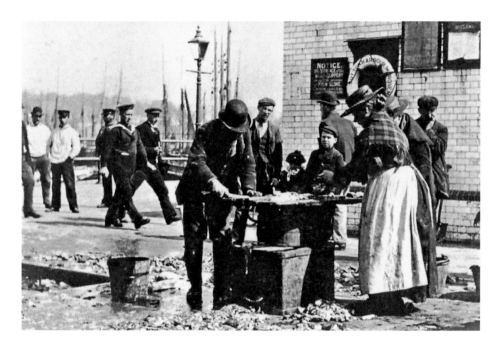

Tom Fry and his wife gutting fish on the Barbican

At one time, the cobbles would be covered in fish guts as the morning's catch was busily cleaned and prepared for the daily fish auctions. An old law stated that, 'ffyshe, flesh, deaded beasts or dogges, cattes and swyne' were not to be thrown off the Quay. It's a very different scene today. Tourists flock to the area and the very busy café, 'Cap'n Jaspers', which was once The White House seen in the original picture, can be seen in the background. The fish market has been moved and now ice cream and fish and chips seems to be the staple diet of visitors to the area.

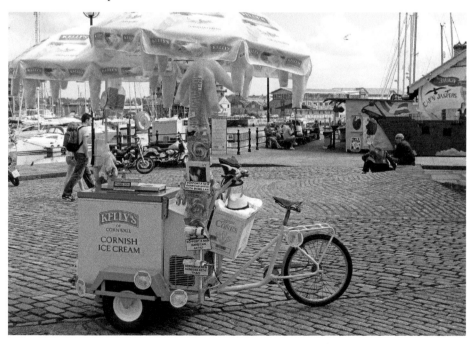

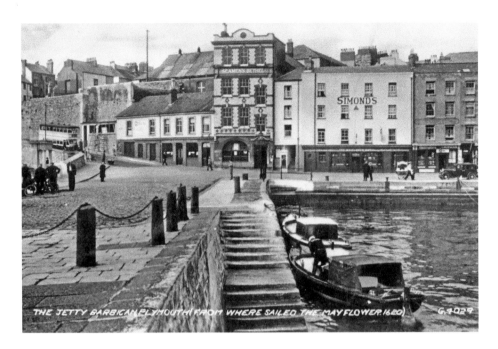

THE JETTY BARBICAN PLYMOUTH FROM WHERE SAILED THE MAYFLOWER 1620)   G.4029

The Jetty, The Barbican

Many of the buildings in the first photograph are still there today. The main difference in these two photographs is that a much more modern building, the Mayflower Visitor Centre, now stands where Simonds once was. Much remains the same apart from more modern cars, vans and boats. The Admiral McBride public house stands on the left of both photographs and within the ladies' toilet is a marker showing the point where the Pilgrim Fathers left from in 1620. The waters of the Quay once came much further back before the jetty was built.

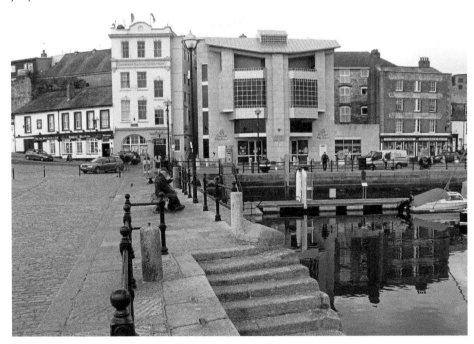

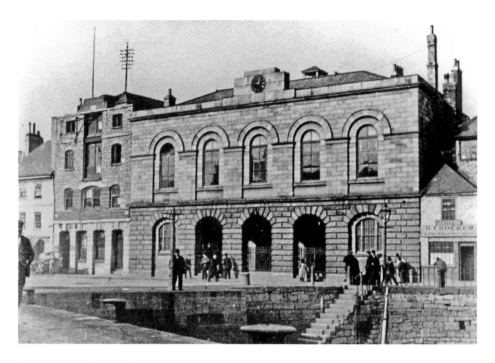

The Customs House, The Barbican

The Customs House was built in 1820 and looks much the same today as it did back then. The original customs house stood across the way and is now a bookshop. Smuggling was once rife and the trade of contraband was very lucrative. To the right of the modern photograph is the popular public house, The Three Crowns.

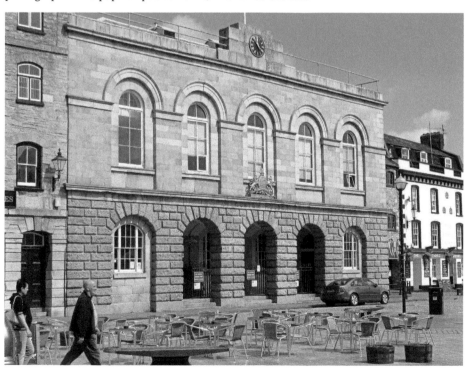

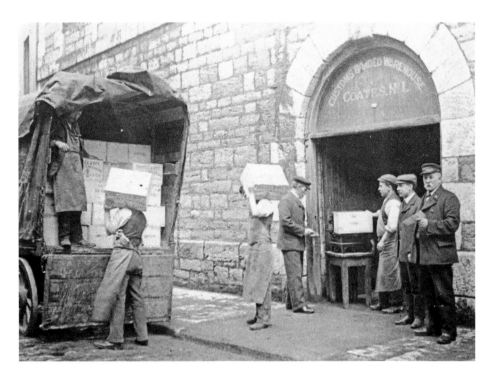

Black Friars Distillery, The Barbican

The building seen here once belonged to Coates and Co who have produced Plymouth Gin since 1793. The top photograph was taken in 1906 and shows a wagon being loaded up with cases of liquor. Today, the same building houses the Barbican Pannier Market which includes a small café. Plymouth Gin is still produced at the nearby distillery which is just across the road.

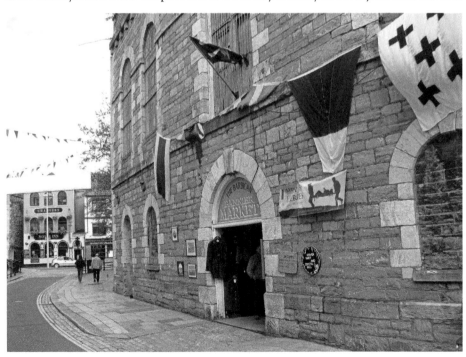

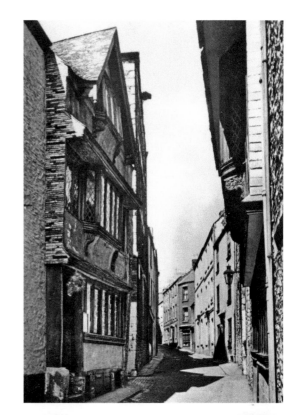

**The Elizabethan House,
New Street, The Barbican**

In 1584, the Mayor of Plymouth, John Sperkes, approved the building of New Street to house people who made their livelihood in and around the harbour. William Hele was the first recorded occupant in 1631. The house is open to the public and also includes an interesting Elizabethan garden. Many buildings in New Street still stand although, in the modern photograph, more recent dwellings can be found on the right.

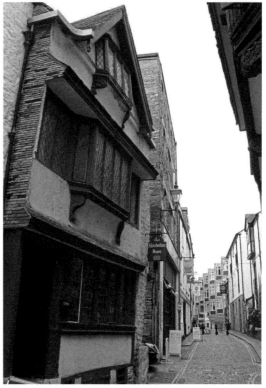

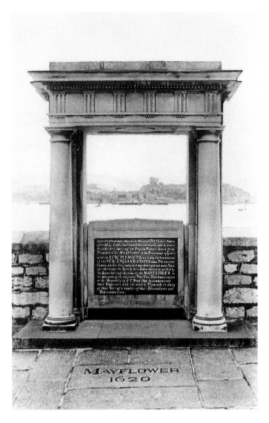

The Mayflower Memorial, The Barbican
These two photographs show the Mayflower Memorial with Mount Batten in the background. In the later photograph, the water taxi to Mount Batten can be seen. Many visitors to the Barbican think that this was the leaving place of the Pilgrim Fathers in 1620 but, as mentioned earlier, this is reclaimed land and the actual leaving place is further back within the nearby Admiral McBride public house.

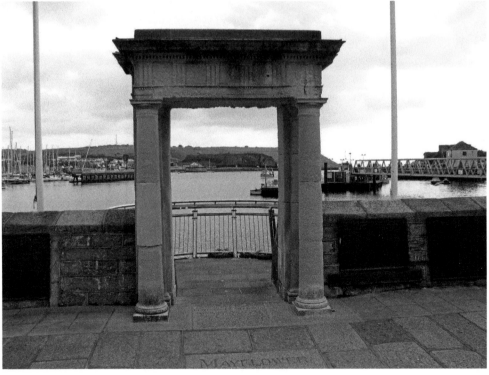

The Merchant's House

Originally built as a wealthy merchant's house in the 1600s, it replaced an earlier house which stood on the same spot in the 1500s. At least three Mayors lived at the house including its first owner, William Parker. In 1972, Plymouth City Council bought the house restoring it to its original glory. Oddly, the modern photograph is more accurate to its original appearance in the 1600s than the older photograph is.

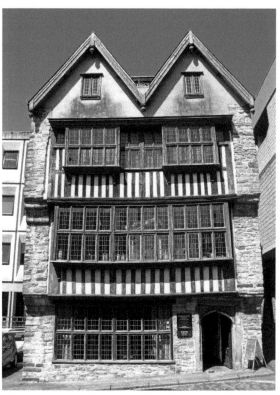

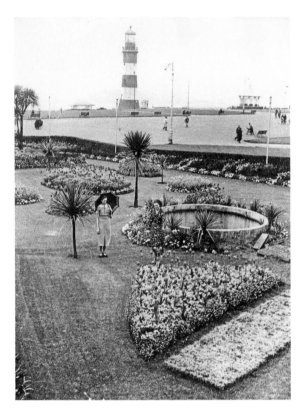

The Hoe Lodge Gardens

Little appears to have changed in these two photographs at first glance. The first photograph was taken in the 1930s and the bandstand to the right of Smeaton's Tower can be seen. Once a popular attraction with regular performances from the Marine Band, it was dismantled in the 1940s for scrap to help with the War Effort.

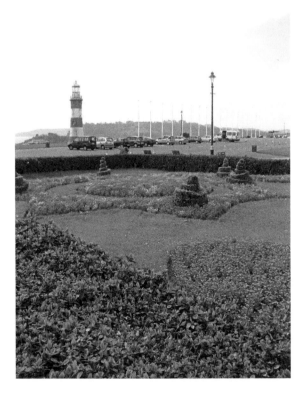

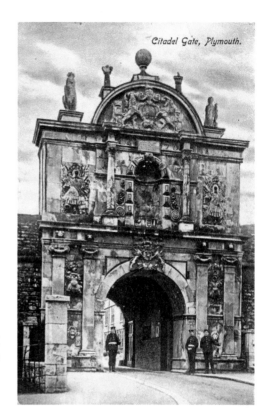

Citadel Gate, Plymouth.

The Citadel Gates

Only the uniforms and weapons seem to have changed between the taking of these two photographs. Work commenced on the Citadel in 1665 under the orders of Charles II who feared an invasion by the Dutch. Canons on the Citadel faced towards the town, as well as out to sea, as a warning to locals who supported Cromwell during the Civil War.

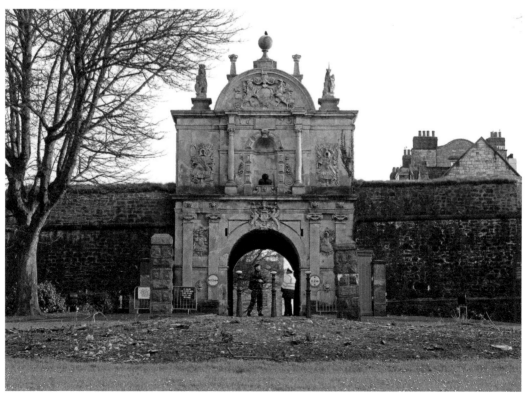

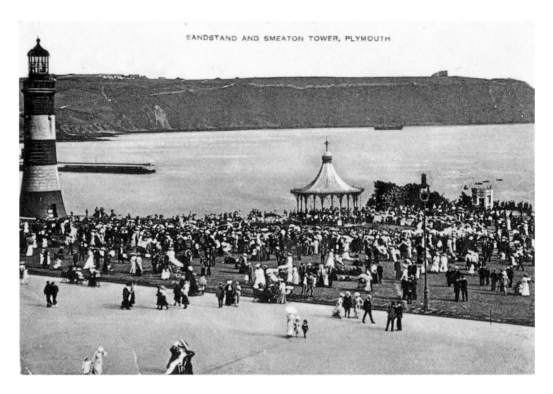

The Bandstand and Smeaton's Tower, The Hoe

A busy scene from about 1910 shows crowds of spectators gathering to watch the band play. The modern photograph shows a more empty Plymouth Hoe with the bandstand long gone. Smeaton's Tower today is painted in its original red and white colour but has had various colour schemes over the years including green and white, the colours of Devon.

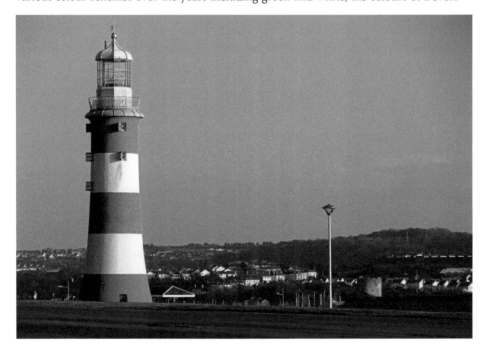

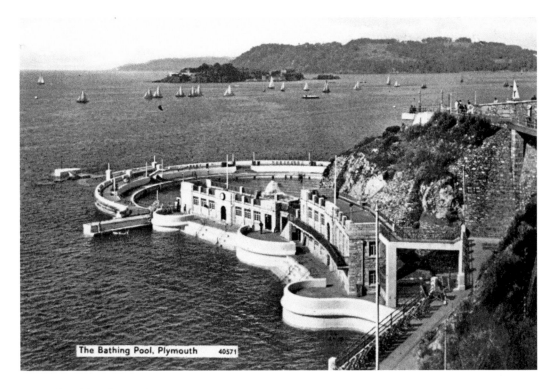

The Bathing Pool, Plymouth   40571

The Lido, Plymouth Hoe

The Lido was opened in 1935 and the first photograph shows an empty scene in the 1950s. Over the years, the pool has been a very busy and popular area but interest in it waned in the 1980s. Today, it has been refurbished and has attracted new visitors but doesn't seem to be as popular as it once was.

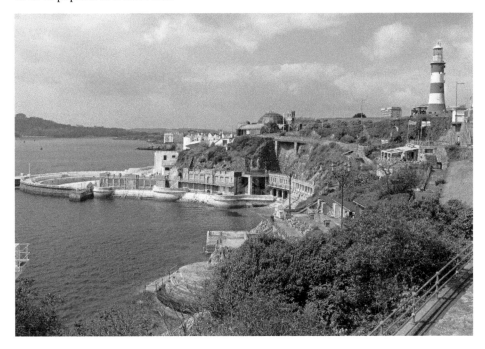

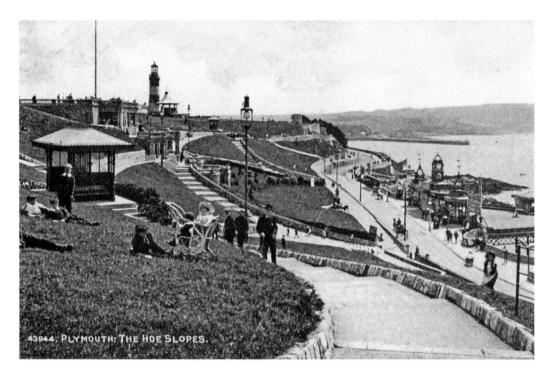

43944 PLYMOUTH: THE HOE SLOPES.

The Hoe Slopes

The older photograph taken in about 1910 shows two landmarks that have long gone, the Pier and the Bandstand. Both were victims of the Second World War. However, much has remained the same in these two photographs with only the fashions and modes of transport having changed. There is one addition in the new photograph and that's the Plymouth Dome attraction in the background. It opened in 1989 but has been closed for many years now.

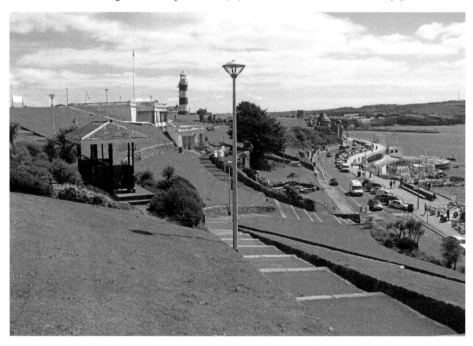

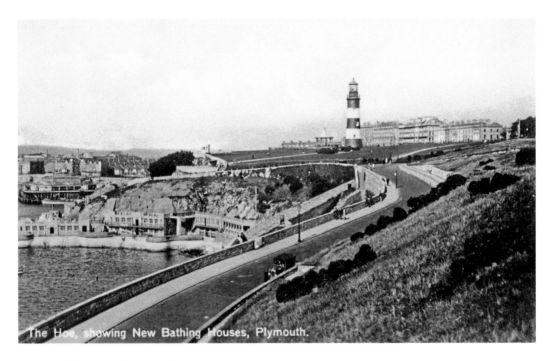

The Hoe, showing New Bathing Houses, Plymouth.

Madeira Road, Plymouth Hoe

These two photographs show how little has changed over the years. The first was taken in the 1930s and a solitary car can be seen on the road. The Pier is still in place in the background and the Lido has yet to be built. The later photograph shows more cars and adverts for Plymouth's Summer Festival appear on the lampposts.

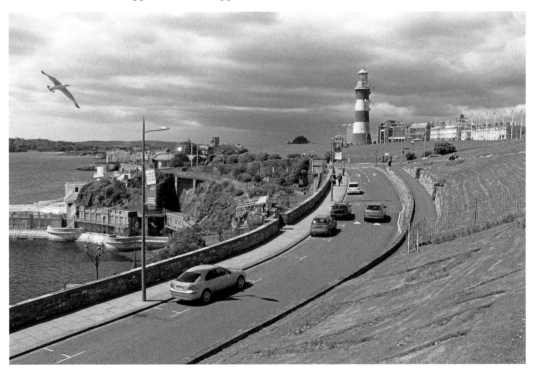

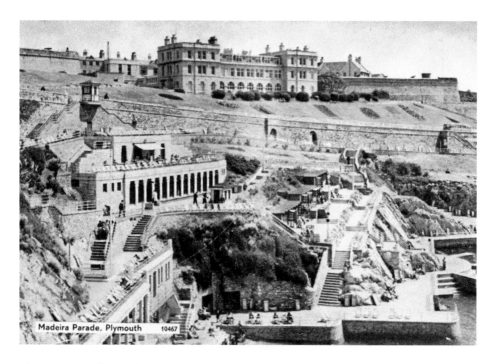

Madeira Parade, Plymouth   10467

The Terraces, Plymouth Hoe

There are subtle changes between these two photographs which at first may be hard to spot. The first photograph was taken in the early 1960s and on the hill can be seen the headquarters of the Marine Biological Association which was opened in 1888. The terraces and beach hut changing rooms remain much the same with the only real noticeable difference being the canopy over the small café near the centre of the picture.

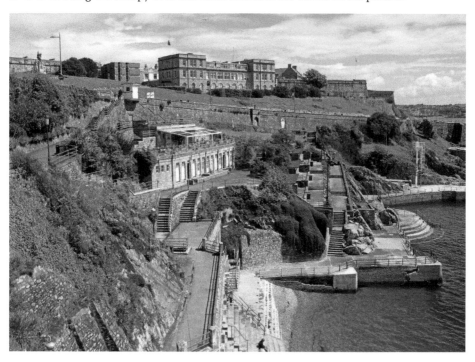

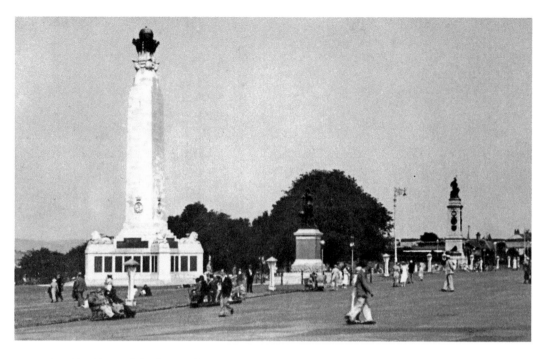

The War Memorial, Plymouth Hoe

The pre-war scene shows many people strolling along the Promenade enjoying the views and good weather. After the Second World War, the War Memorial was extended. The modern photograph shows a very quiet scene with the statue of Sir Francis Drake very much in the forefront.

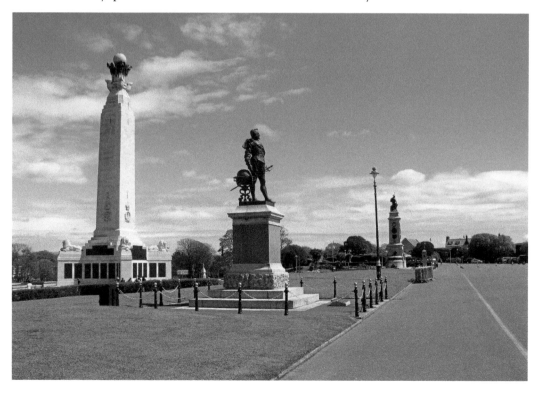

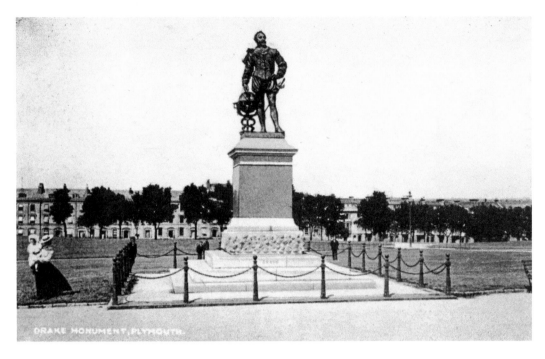

DRAKE MONUMENT, PLYMOUTH.

Drake's Statue, Plymouth Hoe

The early photograph shows a lady in a boater hat with a small child beside the statue of Sir Francis Drake. The statue, which looks out towards Plymouth Sound, was unveiled by Lady Fuller Drake on 14 February 1884. The statue was a copy of the one erected at Tavistock by the Duke of Bedford. Drake had no direct descendants and Lady Fuller was the wife of Sir Francis Fuller Drake who was a descendant of Drake's brother, Thomas.

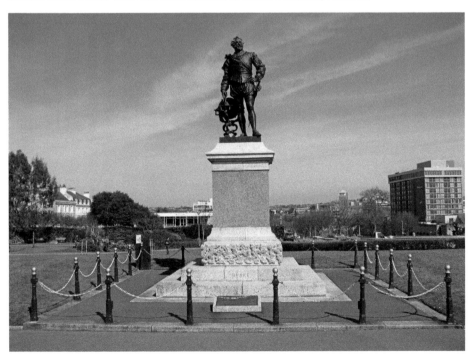

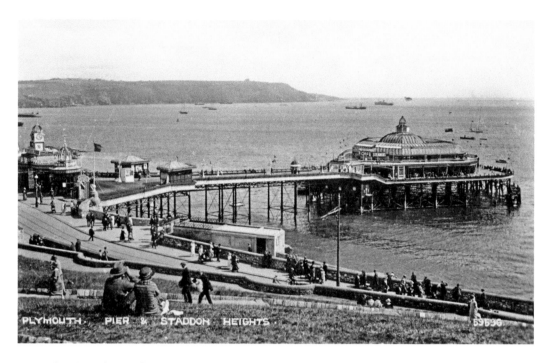

The Pier, Plymouth Hoe

The old photograph from the early 1900s shows Plymouth Pier in all its glory. It was opened in 1884 and proved to be very popular. The Pier contained a stationary and book stall, a reading room, slot machines and a post office. The Pavilion hosted concerts in its large theatre and it was used for roller skating, wrestling, boxing, military shows and dancing. It was a casualty of the bombing of the Second World War and was never rebuilt. Today, looking at the scene, it's hard to imagine that it was ever there.

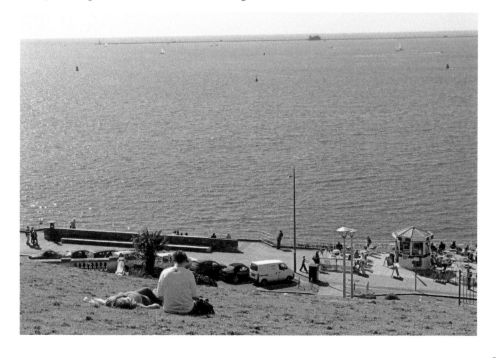

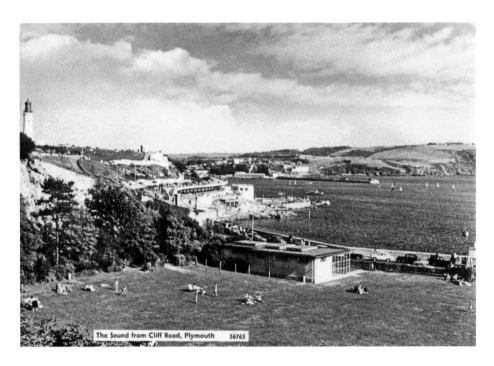

The Sound from Cliff Road, Plymouth   26763

West Hoe

The first photograph was taken in the early 1960s and shows Smeaton's Tower when it was painted white. The following fifty years hasn't brought much change to the area. The trees have grown, partly obscuring the view, and Smeaton's Tower has now been repainted in its original colours. Families still enjoy relaxing on the large grassed area shown especially in the summer months.

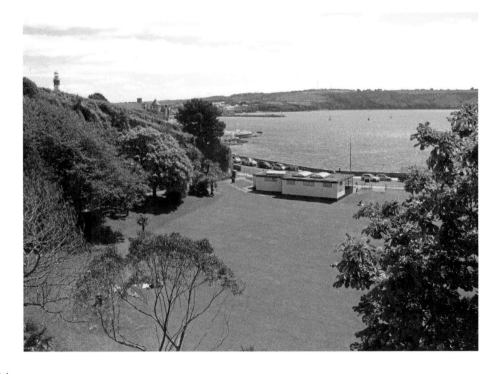

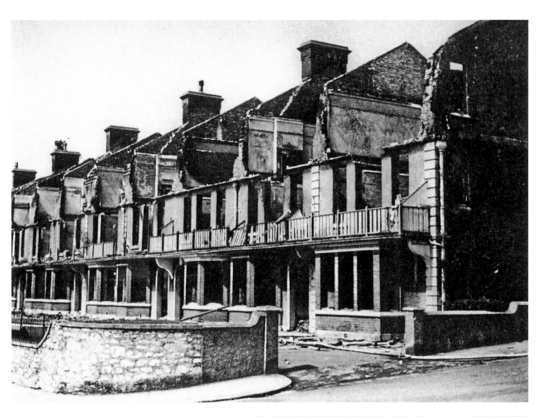

Cliff Road, The Hoe

These houses once stood on Cliff Road and were known simply as The Terrace. They had uninterrupted views across Plymouth Sound and were much sought after. From the first photograph, you can see that they were badly damaged by enemy bombing during the Second Word War. A few years after the War, they were demolished and The Quality Hotel now stands in their place.

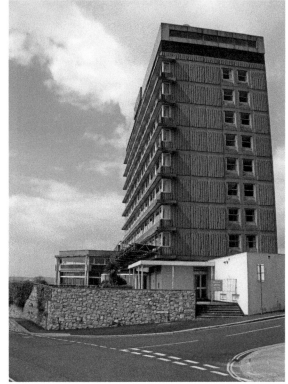

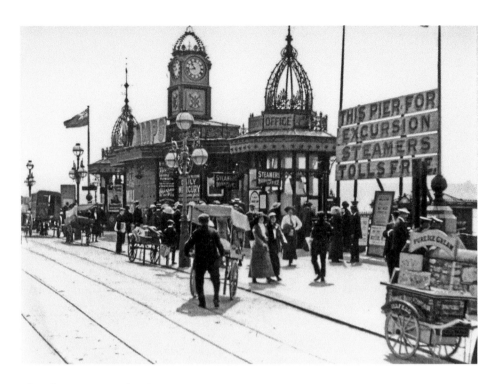

The Pier Entrance, The Hoe

The top photograph taken in the early 1900s shows much activity around the grand Pier entrance. There are many people with handcarts selling their wares, one is selling 'pure ice cream' while another man sells newspapers. There are many adverts including ones for the *Daily Mercury* and others advertising the many steamboat excursions that could be taken from the Pier. Today, it's all gone and a few benches looking out towards the Sound and an ice cream stall take its place.

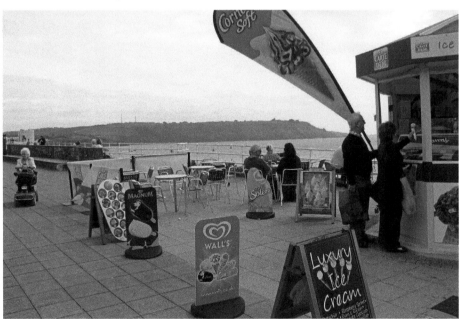

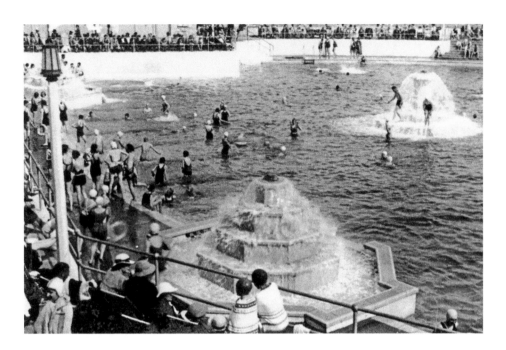

A Busy Lido, Plymouth Hoe

This busy scene shows a packed Lido probably sometime in the late 1930s. It's interesting to see the many people enjoying swimming, as well as lots of spectators including women in fashionable hats. The pool looks much the same today now that it's been refurbished but seems to have lost some of the appeal that it once had.

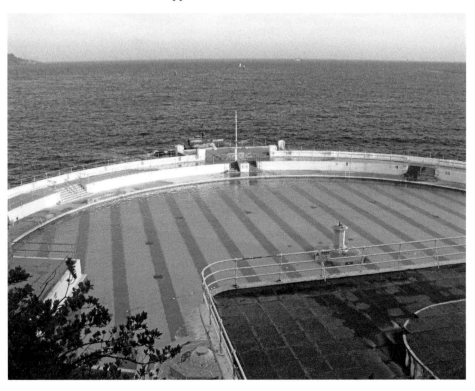

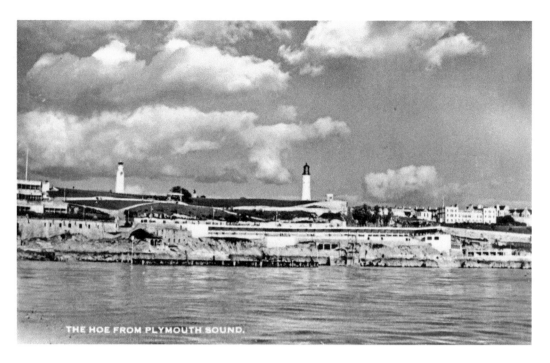

THE HOE FROM PLYMOUTH SOUND.

The Hoe from Plymouth Sound

Fifty years separate these two photographs and the main difference, to the right of the newer photograph, is the Plymouth Dome. The area was once occupied by a very busy café which had views looking right across Plymouth Sound. There are plans to reopen the Dome and to include a restaurant and new attractions sometime in the future.

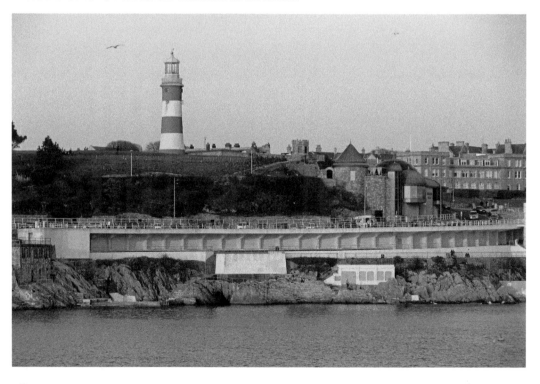

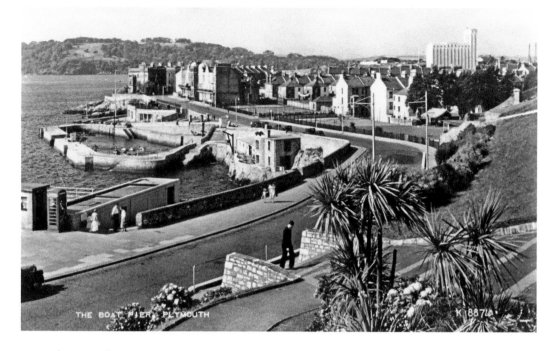

The Boat Pier, West Hoe

The building on the right of the earlier photograph, taken in the 1950s, is the now demolished grain silo at Millbay. Behind the small quay, new apartment buildings have been built in keeping with the original buildings that already stood there. These were completed in the 1980s. It's interesting to see, after almost sixty years, that the red phone box on the left of both photographs, still stands in exactly the same place.

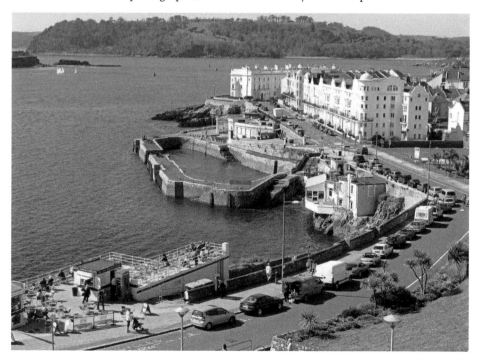

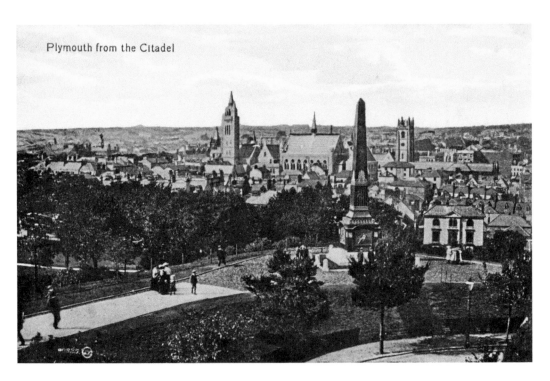

Plymouth from the Citadel

Plymouth from the Citadel

The view from the early 1900s shows Plymouth as it once was before the heavy bombing of the Second World War. Also featured in the photograph is the Boer War Memorial which was unveiled on 8 August 1903 by Lady Audrey Buller. In the later photograph, many more modern buildings can be seen in the background.

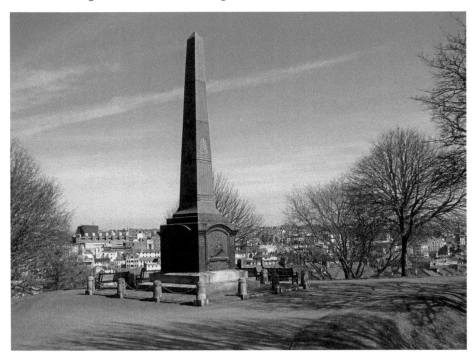

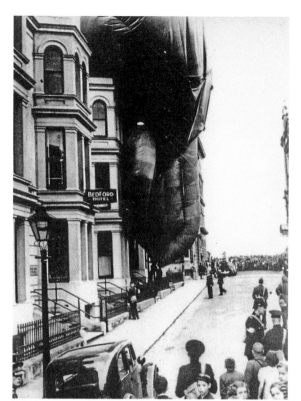

The Strathmore Hotel, Plymouth Hoe
The wartime photograph shows a
barrage balloon that has crashed onto
the Strathmore Hotel in Elliot Street.
Little has changed between these two
photographs and the hotel is still open
for business today. The road leads up
to the Hoe and also towards Elliot
Terrace which was once the home of
Lord and Lady Astor.

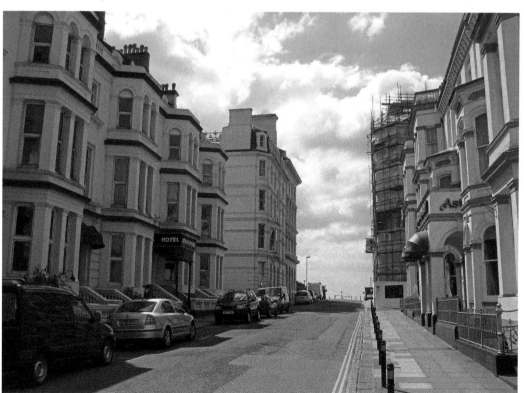

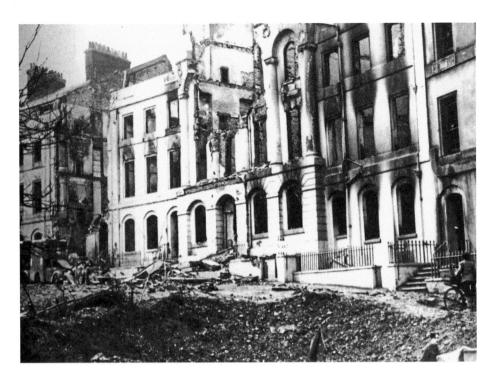

The Crescent

During the Second World War, the Crescent took a direct hit which caused extensive damage which destroyed the Westminster and Hacker's Hotels. Here, a lady with a bicycle surveys the destruction. It was later rebuilt in the same style and today houses solicitors, architects and medical practitioners.

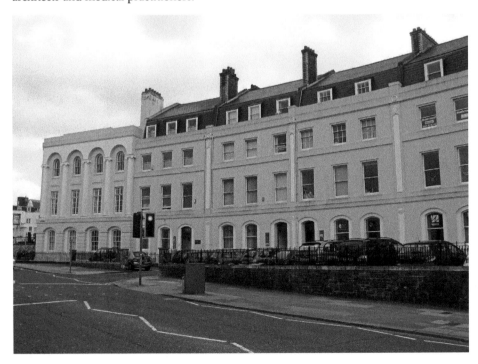

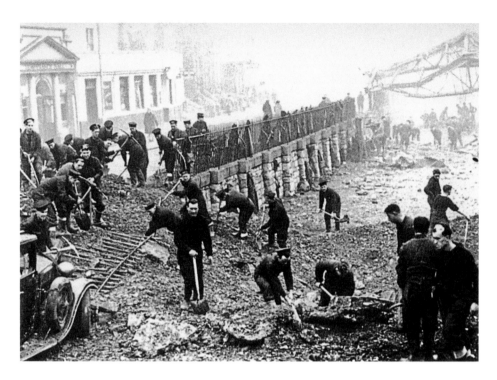

Millbay Station

Millbay Station was another casualty of the Second World War. It was first opened in 1849 and proved to be very busy. It was bombed in 1941 and was closed to passengers shortly afterwards. Nowadays, the land is occupied by the Pavilions, an entertainment centre. Incidentally, the posts seen in the modern photograph are from the original station.

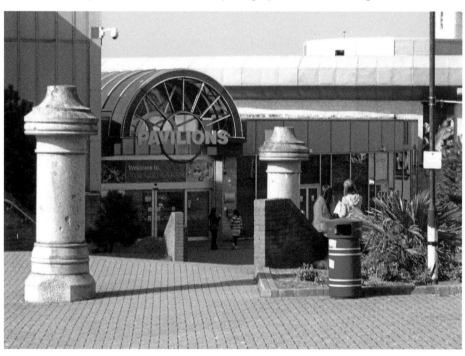

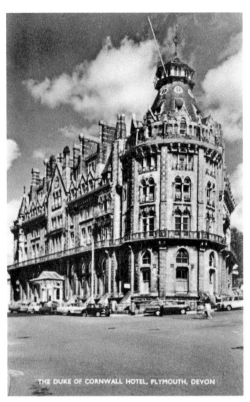

THE DUKE OF CORNWALL HOTEL, PLYMOUTH, DEVON

The Duke of Cornwall Hotel
The hotel was opened opposite Millbay Station in 1862 to cater for the many rail passengers who would later be travelling onwards by train or travelling on one of the many passenger liners that called regularly into the city. It narrowly escaped bombing in the Second World War and remains much the same today.

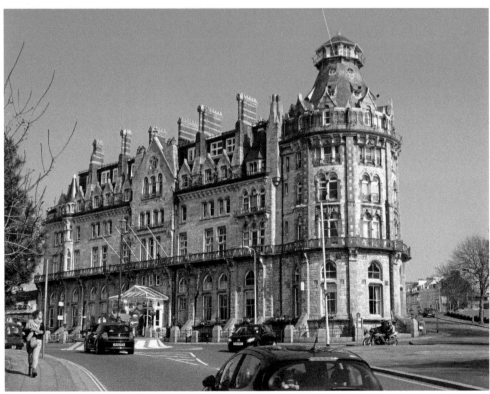

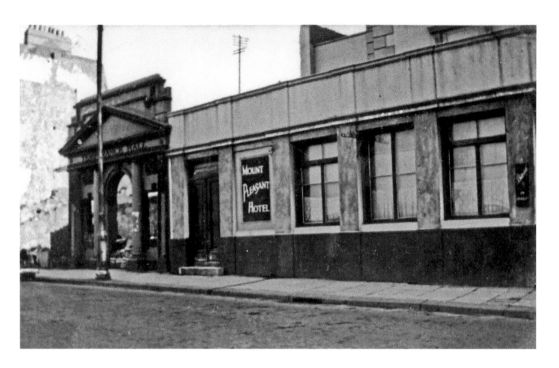

The Mount Pleasant Hotel

The Mount Pleasant Hotel stood next to the Duke of Cornwall Hotel but, as can be seen from the photograph, didn't fare so well during the bombing in the Second World War. Amazingly, it wasn't demolished but was rebuilt in much the same style as it was originally. It is now a public house but almost looks out of place amongst its taller neighbours.

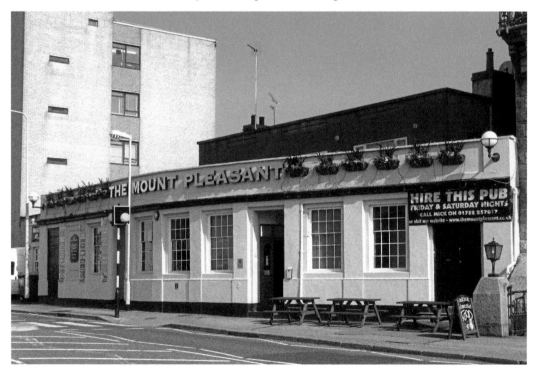

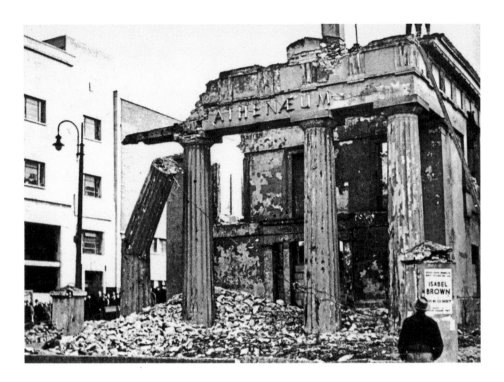

The Athenaeum

The Athenaeum was designed by John Foulston and the foundation stone was laid in 1818. Bombing on the 21 April 1941 totally destroyed the building taking with it some of the oldest prehistoric relics found in the city including remains of prehistoric rhinoceroses, horses, oxen, and deer. The newer Athenaeum was rebuilt in the same location and opened in 1961.

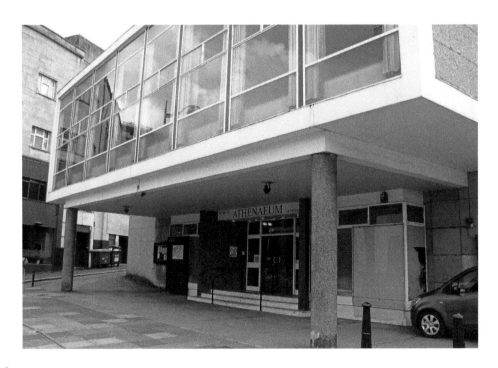

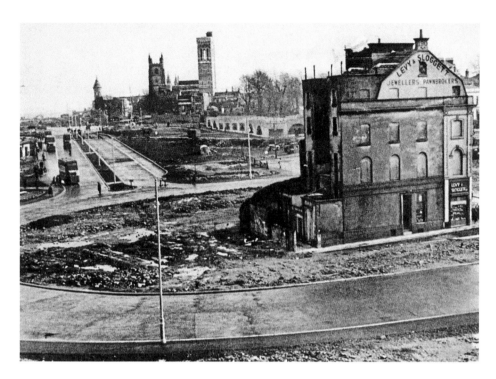

Building of Royal Parade

When reconstruction started in Plymouth after the War, the premises of Levy & Sloggett, a former pawnbrokers and jewellers, found itself isolated on Derry's Cross roundabout. The building was finally removed in 1956. Today, Royal Parade and the City Centre have changed greatly and there are no signs of the total devastation that once took place there.

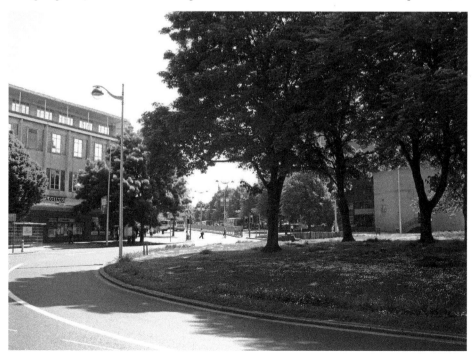

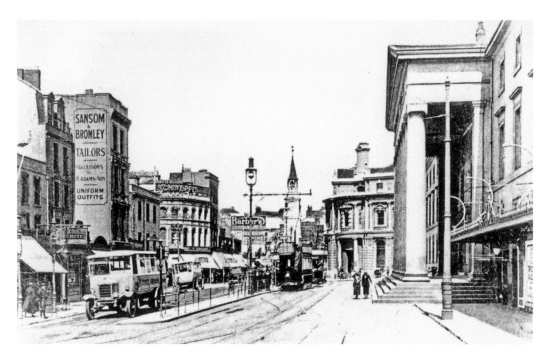

The Theatre Royal, George Street

This lovely old photograph shows the Theatre Royal in George Street. Although a magnificent building, it was demolished in 1937 to make way for a purpose built cinema, The Royal, which later became the ABC in 1958. The cinema still stands and is adjacent to the multi-storey car park that can be seen on the right of the recent photograph. The only recognisable features today are Derry's Clock and the old bank beside it which is now a public house.

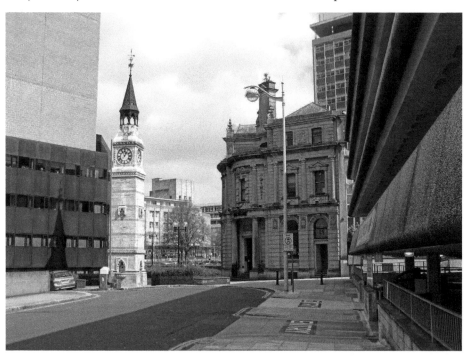

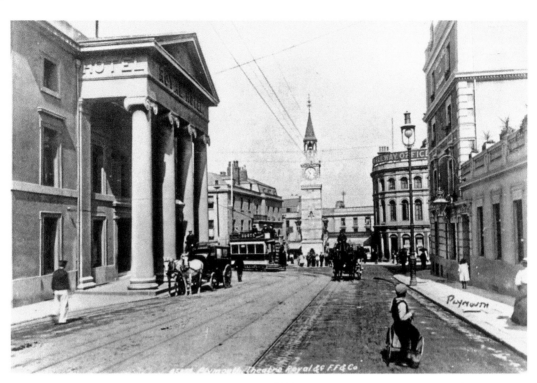

Derry's Clock and the Royal Hotel
The Royal Hotel has now long gone as well as many of the other buildings in the original photograph. Today, Derry's Clock and the Bank public house are overshadowed by a multi-storey car park on the left and the Theatre Royal, built in the 1980s, in the background.

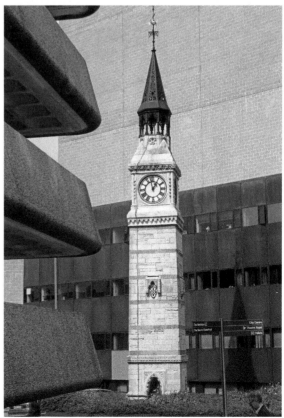

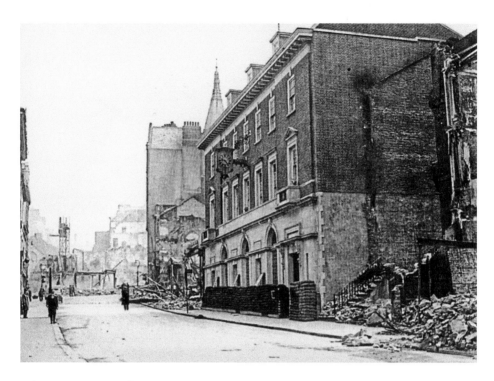

Leicester Harmsworth House

Once, for many years, the offices of the *Western Morning News*, Leicester Harmsworth House was one of the few buildings to survive the Blitz of 1941. When the city was rebuilt after the War, the building remained in place while the new city was built around it. Today, although drastically altered, it houses the premises of Waterstone's Bookstore.

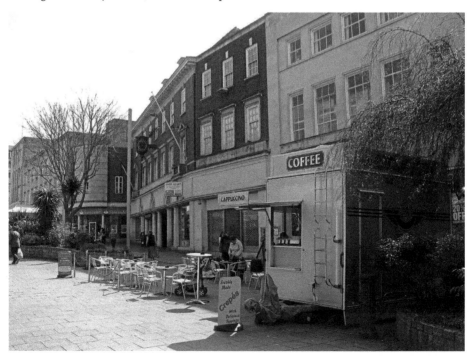

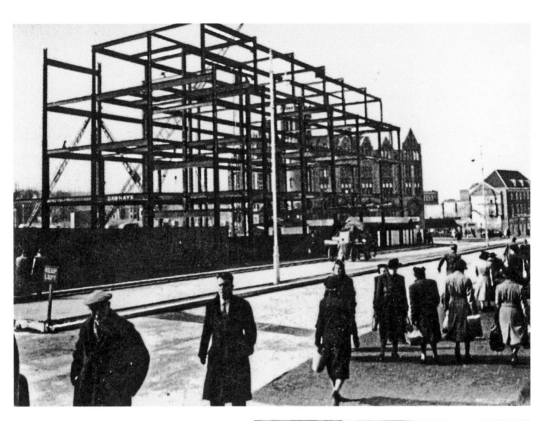

New George Street

The old photograph shows the reconstruction of the city and the building of what was to become the city's new departmental stores. In the distance can be seen Leicester Harmsworth House. After the devastation of the Second World War, the new Plymouth was seen as being very modern. Shops have come and gone but much of the City Centre remains the same as when it was built back in the late 1940s and early 1950s.

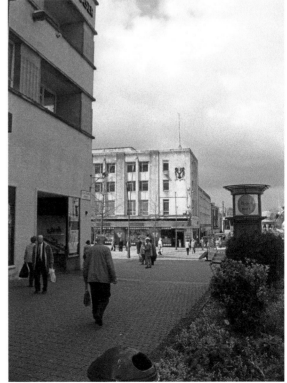

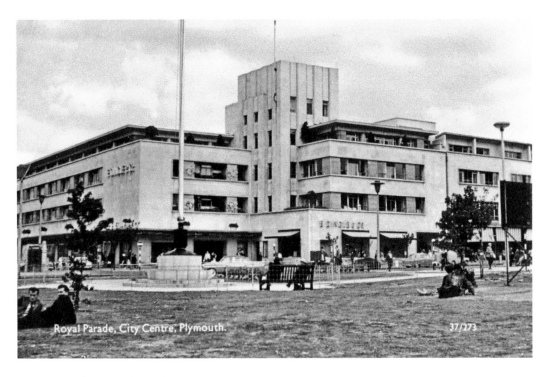

Royal Parade, City Centre, Plymouth.   37/273

E. Dingle's, Royal Parade

The old view shows E. Dingle's new premises on Royal Parade in the 1950s. In June 1951, Dingle's signed a ninety-nine year lease and traded for many years before being bought out by the House of Fraser in 1971. Only recently has the Dingle's name been removed from the building, as can be seen in the recent photograph.

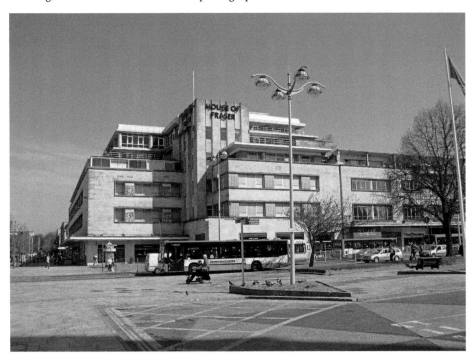

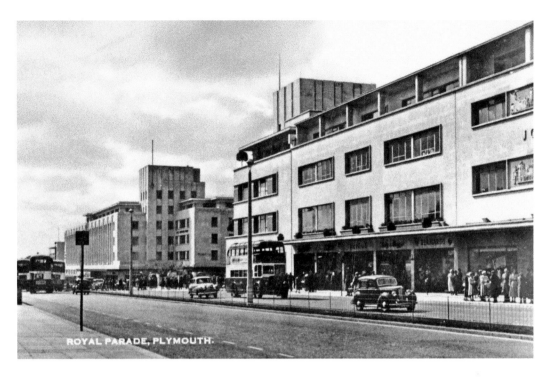

Royal Parade

A 1950s postcard shows Royal Parade when it was relatively new with few cars and several double decker buses. Today, it's a very busy area with much traffic including many single decker buses taking people all over the city. The buildings, however, have seen little change over the years.

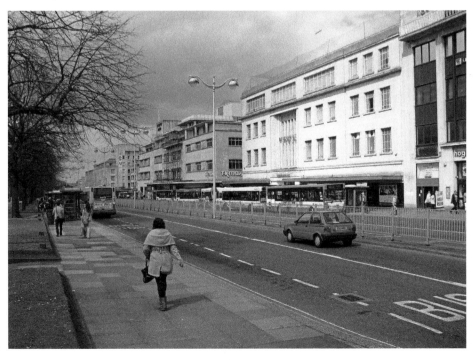

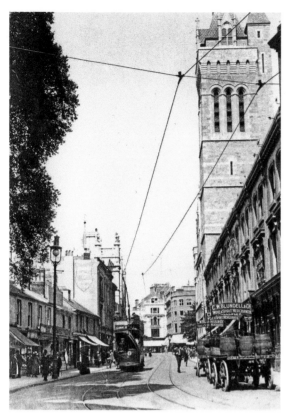

The Guildhall
The first photograph shows Plymouth as it once was before the German bombs rained down. This scene would be almost unrecognisable today if it wasn't for the tower of the Guildhall on the right of the photograph. It's lovely to see the old streets, trams and horse drawn carts. The area now forms Armada Way which leads from the Hoe towards the City Centre.

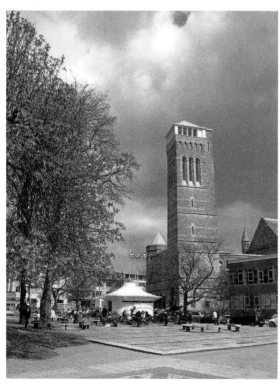

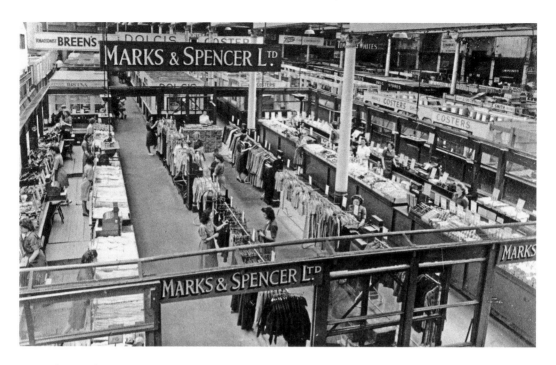

The Market

There has been a market in Plymouth since 1253. When the city was devastated by heavy bombing in 1941, many of the larger businesses moved into the Pannier Market. These included Marks & Spencer, Costers and Boots. Work started on the present market in 1952 and was completed in 1959. The later colour photograph shows the market as it is today, still as busy as ever.

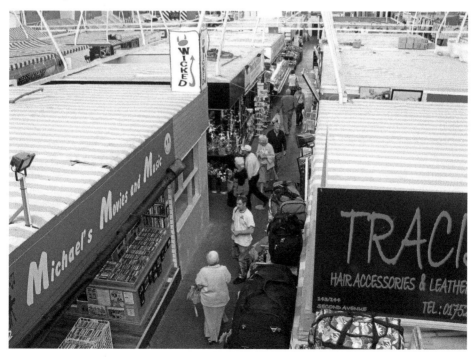

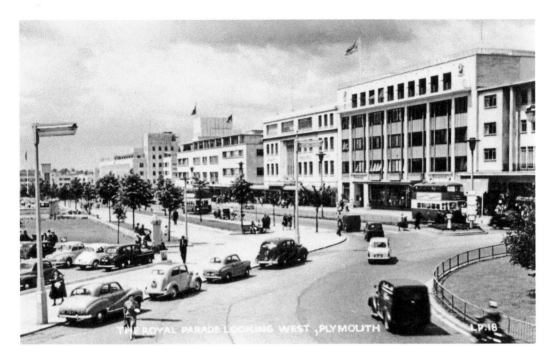

The top of Royal Parade

The first photograph shows the newly built shopping centre in the 1950s. There are many cars and buses travelling up and down Royal Parade. Before the War, the streets were narrow and soon became congested. Today's scene appears emptier but the traffic into the city has increased immensely. There is little change apart from the newer lampposts. However, if the tree wasn't so big on the left hand side of the photograph, the Civic Centre, built in the 1960s, would also be able to be seen.

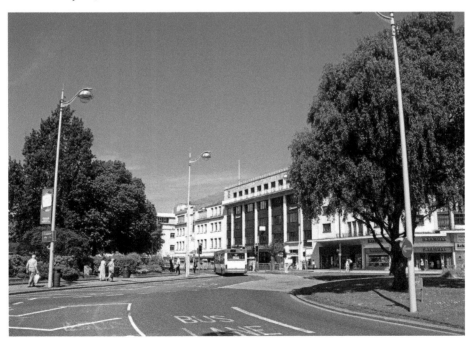

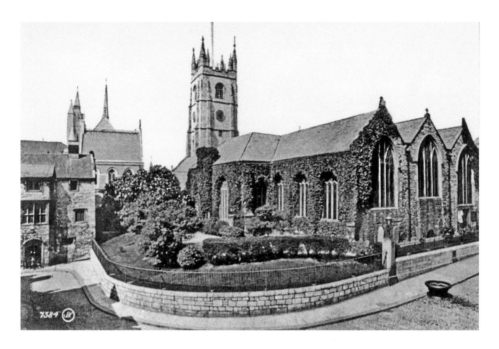

St Andrew's Church

Beside St Andrew's in the first picture is the Prysten House which dates from the fifteenth century. Looking at the two photographs, it would appear that not much has changed over the years but during the War, St Andrew's was bombed and remained without a roof for many years.

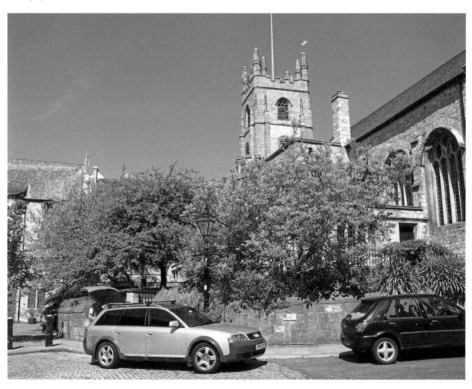

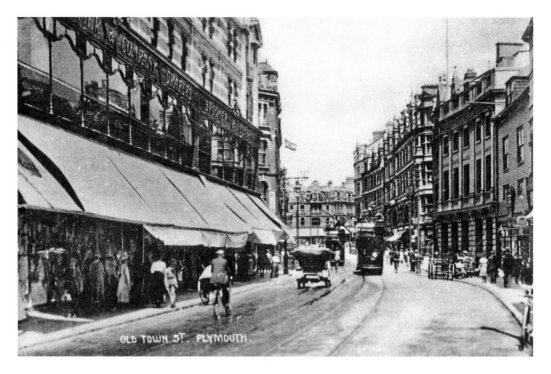

Old Town Street

With the rebuilding of the City Centre, little remains today of Old Town Street. In the later photograph, the Post Office can be seen on the right of the picture and from here to the new Drake Circus Shopping Mall is all that is left of Old Town Street. The original street was once very busy with many shops including photographers, jewellers, drapers and tobacconists.

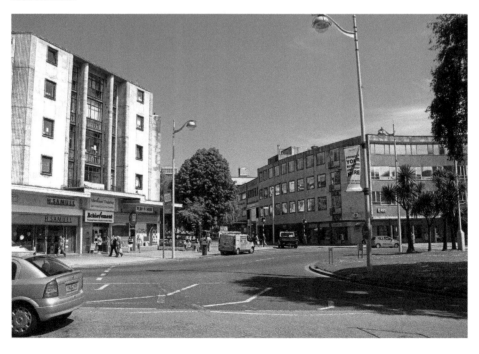

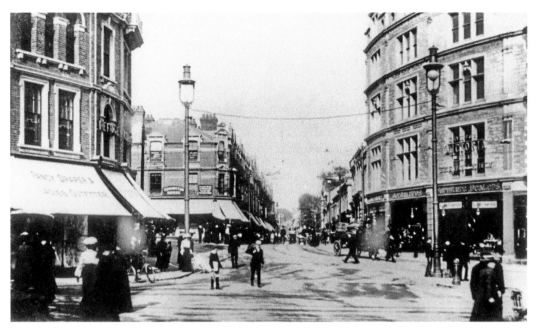

Drake Circus

Drake Circus has seen many changes over the years. Once famous for its old buildings and the Guinness Clock, which many residents relied on to tell the time. The area was demolished in 1967 to build a new shopping centre which opened in 1971. In 2004, the area was redeveloped again and the new Drake Circus Shopping Mall was built to mixed reactions. It opened in October 2006.

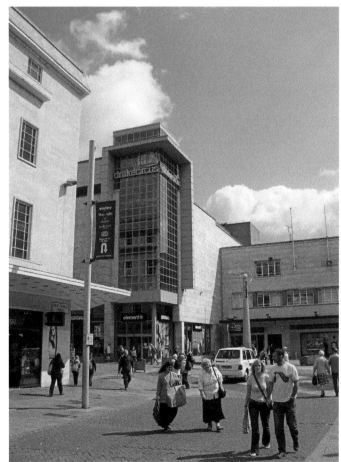

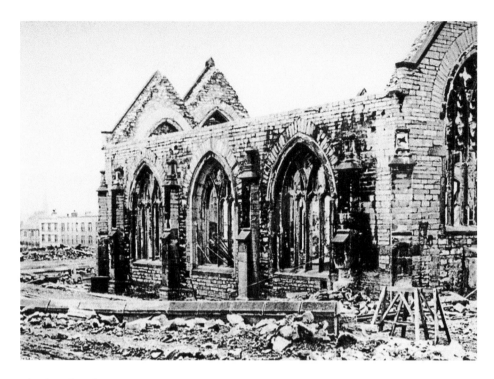

Charles Church

The bomb-damaged ruins of Charles Church stand on the roundabout at Charles Cross as a monument to the civilians who died in the Second World War. Today, it's dwarfed by the new, rather odd, Drake Circus Shopping Mall behind it. For many years, a multi-storey car park stood where the Mall stands today.

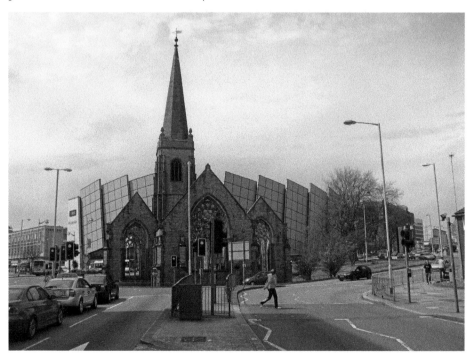

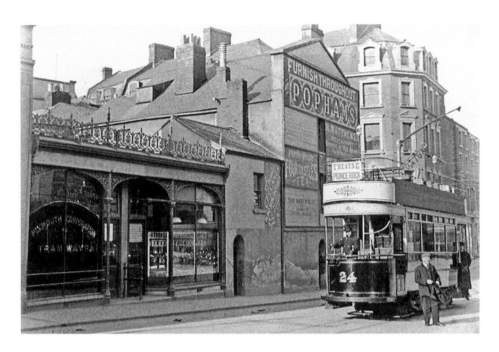

Goulds in Ebrington Street

Goulds has been an Army Surplus Store in Ebrington Street since 1955 and is very well known in the city. The earlier photograph shown here includes a lovely old tram and the driver appears to have stopped to pose for the camera. There are many interesting adverts on the walls of the buildings including ones for Pophams, G. P. Skinner, H. Matthews' Restaurant, Four Castles Tea and a production at the local theatre.

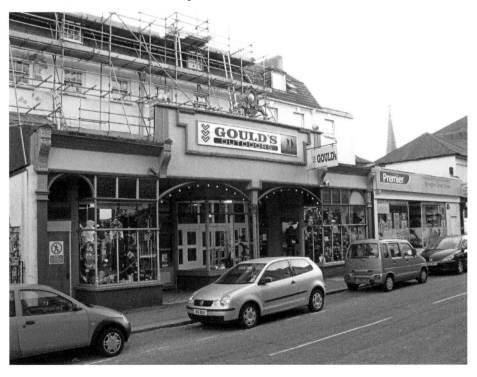

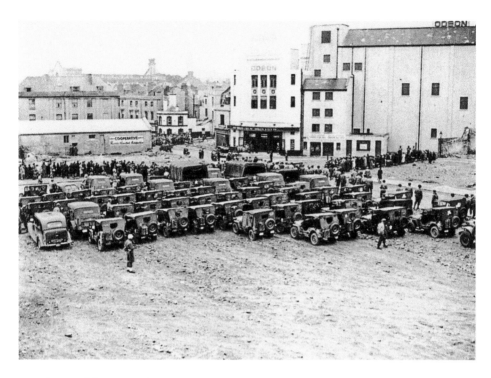

American Soldiers at Union Street

The older photograph shows American troops who were station in Plymouth in the early 1940s. This piece of bomb damaged land remained much the same until the 1980s. Over the years, it has housed an open car park and was host to the popular open-air market in the 1970s. In the 1980s, a Sainsbury's Homebase was built on the land but this was later taken over by Toys R Us.

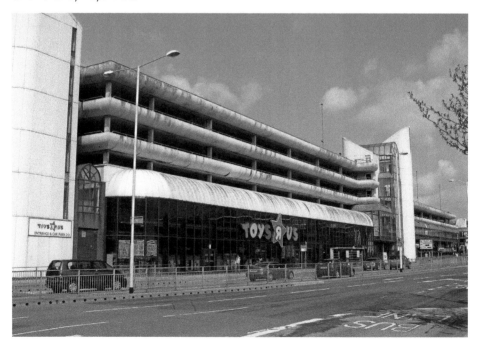

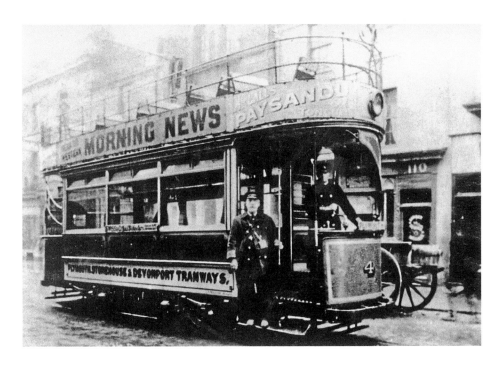

A Tram, Union Street

This lovely old tram is outside 110 Union Street which, unfortunately, no longer exists. Much of Union Street was bombed during the Second World War but many interesting buildings remained even up until the 1980s. In the 1970s, it was the home to clubs, pubs and interesting second hand shops. Today, the area where the original photograph was taken would be in the gap after the first lot of buildings shown on the left of the modern photograph.

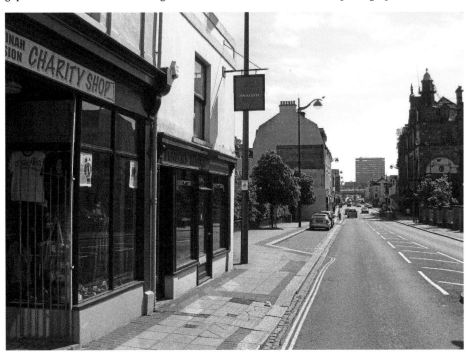

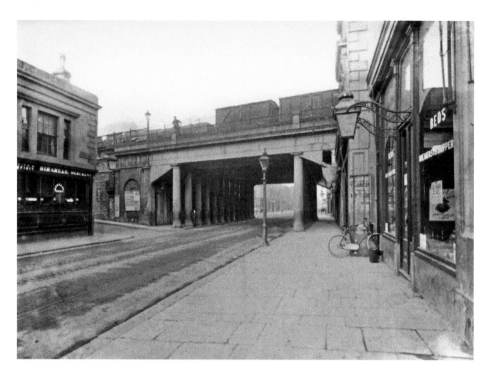

Union Street Arch

The early photograph showing Union Street arch was taken at the beginning of the 1900s. The arch carried rail traffic from the nearby Millbay Station and was eventually removed in the 1970s. In its place today is a walkway leading from the Toys R Us building and car park over to the Pavilions entertainments centre.

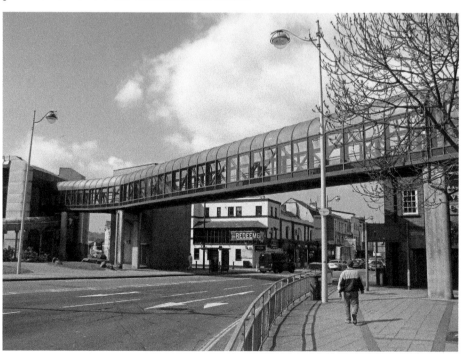

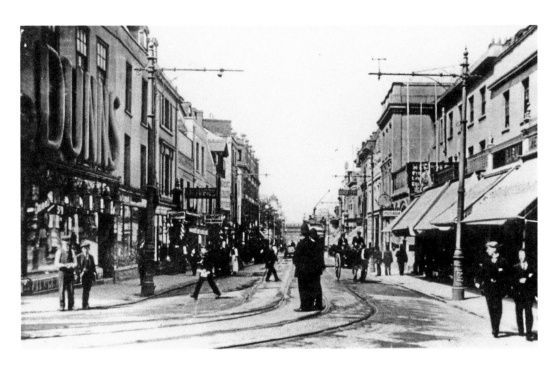

Union Street

This busy scene shows Union Street in the early 1900s and also shows all the wonderful buildings that once stood there. Much has changed over the years. The ornate Palace Theatre, where Houdini and Laurel and Hardy once played, can be seen on the left of the modern photograph. It has been closed for many years now. Much of the character of the old Union Street has either been bombed, demolished or neglected.

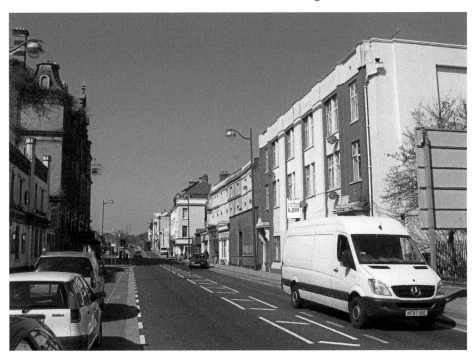

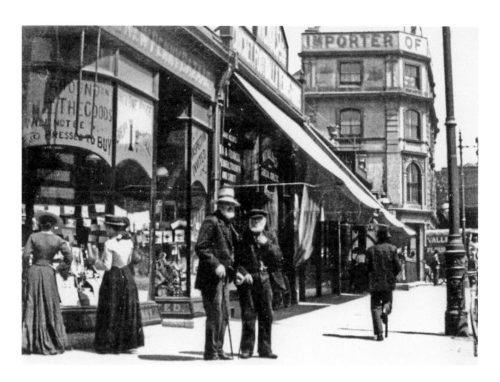

Men Talking, Union Street

The original photograph shows the view looking towards the Union Street arch with the town centre in the distance. The area has changed completely nowadays. The shops and buildings are long gone and their replacements are worse for wear.

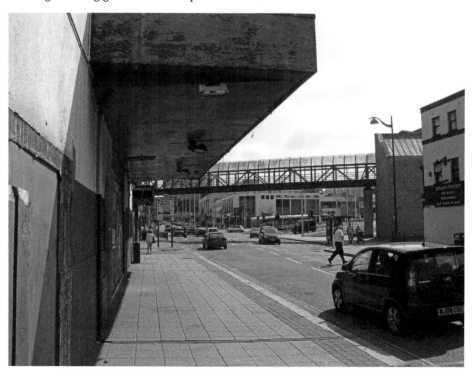

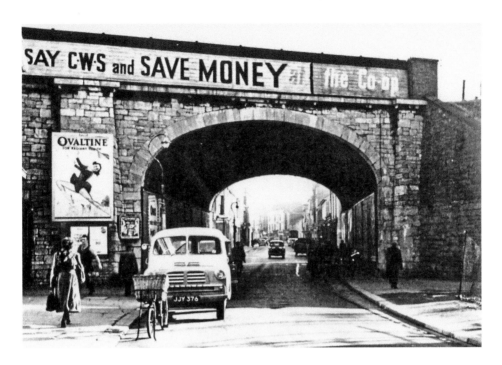

The King Street Arch

Organ grinders with monkeys, chestnut sellers, butchers and rabbit catchers all plied their trade from underneath the King Street arch in the early 1900s. A man on stilts would tap on windows to announce forthcoming events such as the fair or the circus. The arch was pulled down in the 1970s which completely altered the look of the area. New flats were built as well as the building on the right which now houses Toys R Us.

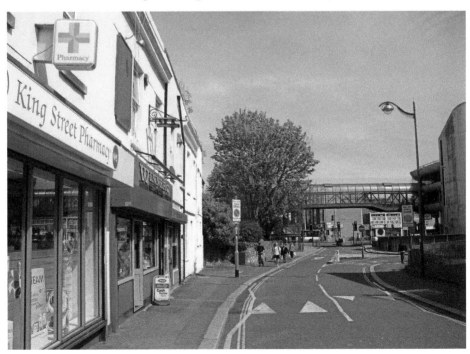

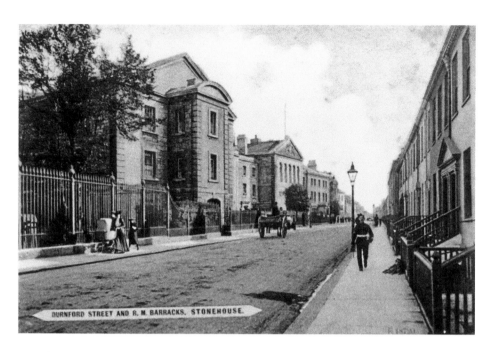

DURNFORD STREET AND R. M. BARRACKS, STONEHOUSE.

Durnford Street

Once the home of doctors, merchants and the well-off. Sir Arthur Conan Doyle assisted at a medical practice at Durnford Street and Sherlock Holmes was said to be based on his colleague, Dr Budd. On the left of both photographs can be seen the Royal Marines Barracks and, apart from the traffic, much remains the same.

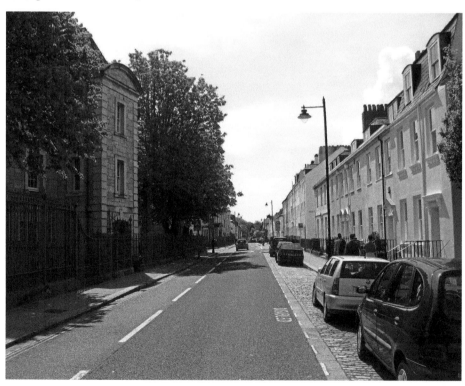

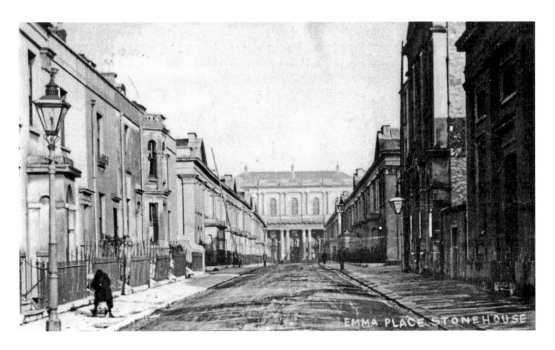

Emma Place, Stonehouse

In the distance, in the first photograph, can be seen Stonehouse Town Hall which was erected between 1849 and 1850. It was destroyed in the Second World War. The buildings on the left have now all gone but many of the buildings on the right of the photograph still remain.

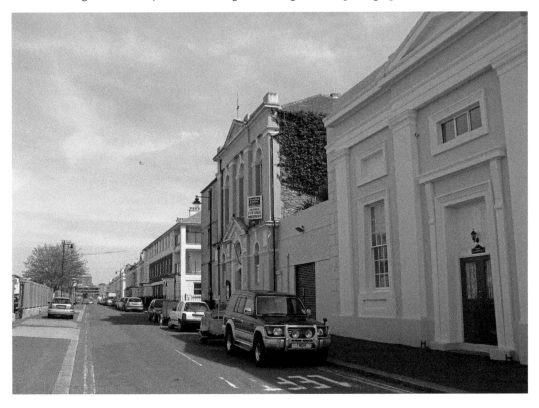

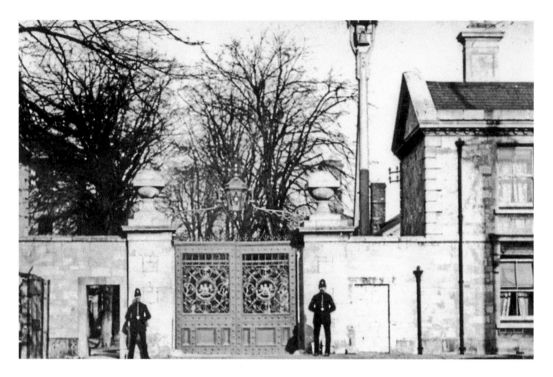

The Royal Naval Hospital, Stonehouse

Today, the Royal Naval Hospital is now Millfields, an upmarket gated community with their own security guards. Work started on the hospital in the late 1700s and it treated patients up until the 1990s. There are some changes to the entrance but much of the outside of the buildings remain the same.

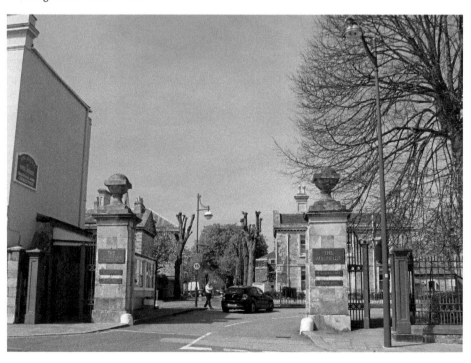

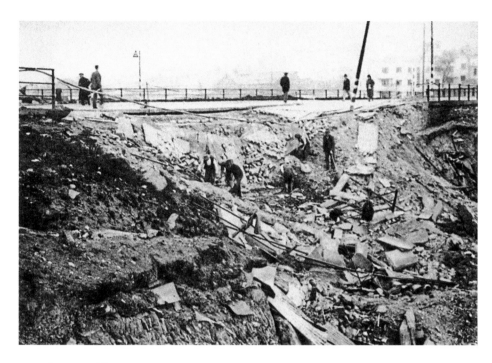

Stonehouse Bridge

The first photograph shows Stonehouse Bridge destroyed by bombing in the Second World War. It was once a toll bridge and was known then as Ha'penny Bridge. In 1909, Houdini leapt from the bridge in chains into the waters below and managed to free himself in front of a large crowd who had gathered to watch. Today, the rebuilt Stonehouse Bridge is as busy as it ever was, taking much traffic daily into the City Centre.

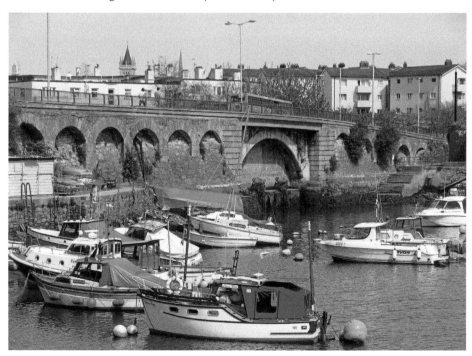

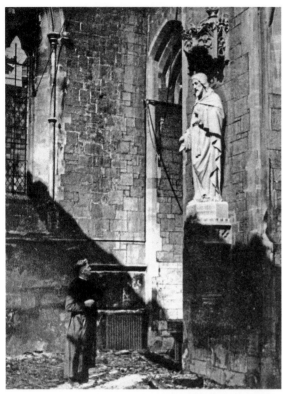

St Peter's Church, Wyndham Square
Extensively damaged during the War, St Peter's Church in Wyndham Square was rebuilt in 1955. Between 2004 and 2007, the church was renovated and the results are very impressive. Many of the nearby properties are Grade II listed and, during the last century, some were reported to be haunted.

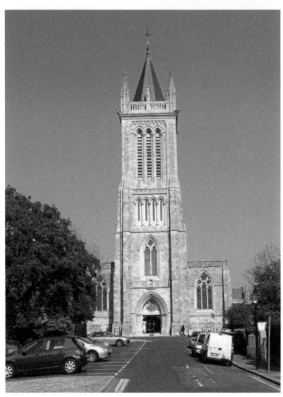

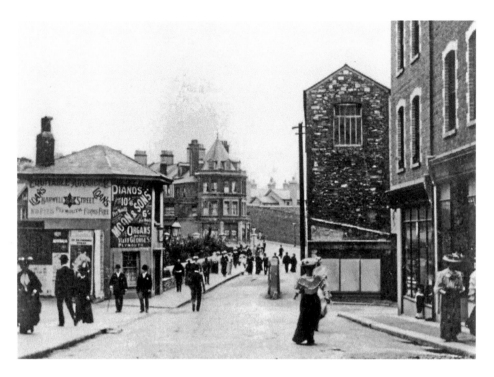

Millbridge

The building on the left of the first photograph was once a toll house and tolls were collected up until 1924. Millbridge was originally built in 1525 by Sir Piers Edgcumbe and Stonehouse Creek once flowed past the area in the distance. Then known as the Deadlake, the land was reclaimed in the late 1800s and is now Victoria Park. The building in the distance and the buildings on the right of the photograph still remain.

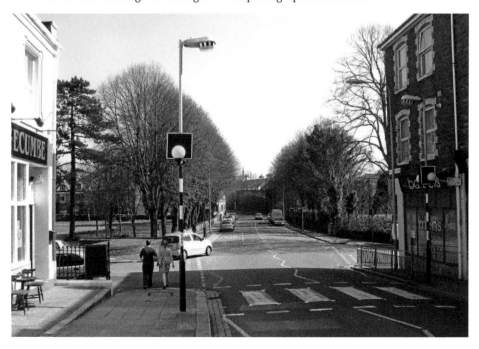

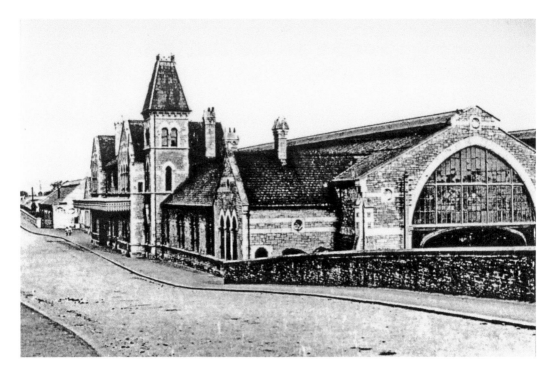

Devonport Railway Station, Kings Road
The station at Kings Road opened in 1876 and was used extensively. It was damaged by bombing in the Second World War but remained in use after the War until it was closed in 1964. It was eventually demolished and the College of Further Education was built in its place.

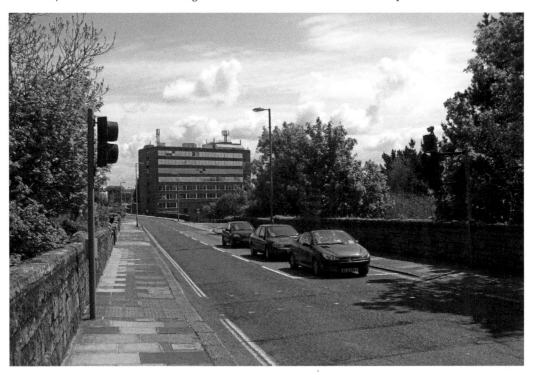

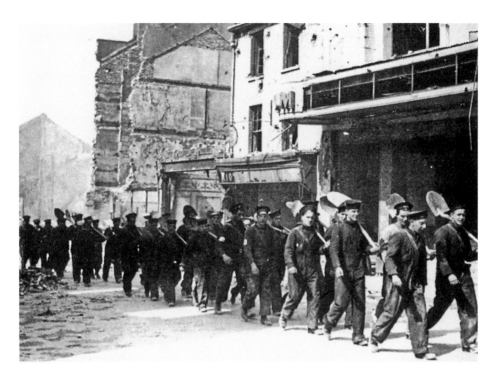

The Forum, Fore Street, Devonport

Once a popular cinema in the middle of Fore Street, the whole area changed dramatically with the bombing of the Second World War. Much of Fore Street was damaged or destroyed and the bottom half of the street was later enclosed within the Dockyard. Today, the Forum is a bingo hall with little remaining of the street that once surrounded it.

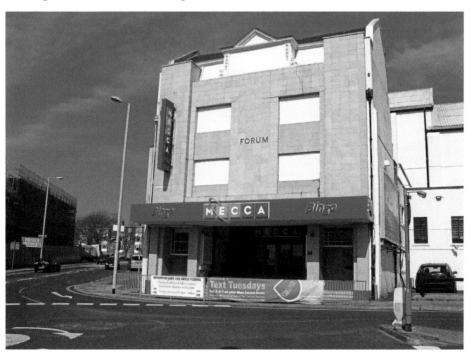

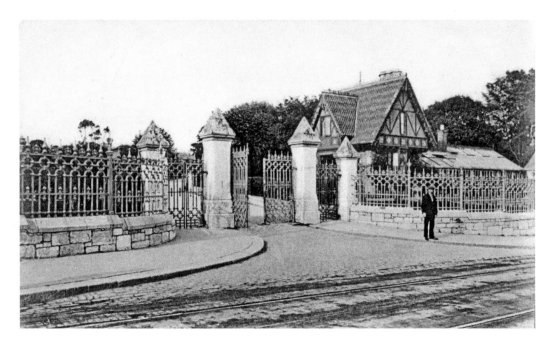

The Swiss Lodge, Stoke Road, Devonport Park

The Swiss Lodge and Devonport Park have recently been renovated but for many years, the Lodge lay in a state of disrepair. It was designed by Alfred Norman of Devonport and the park was opened to the public in 1895. Trams regularly passed by this way and the tramlines can be seen in the original photograph.

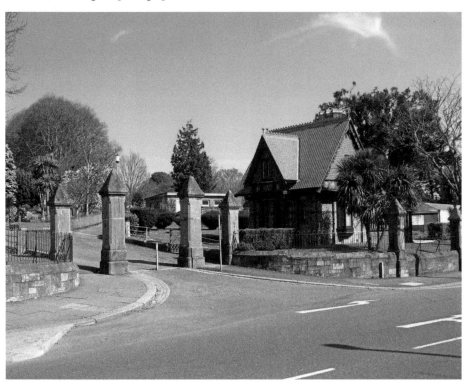

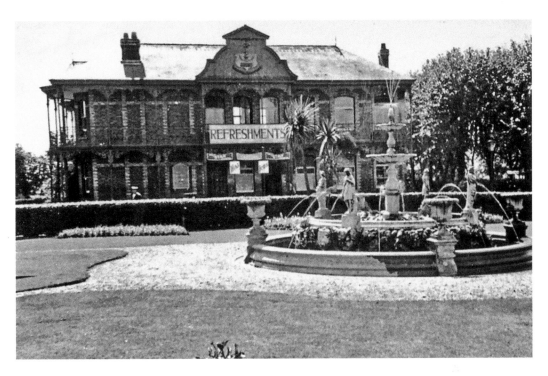

Higher Lodge, Devonport Park

Higher Lodge within Devonport Park can be seen in both of these photographs. Today, it's a care home for the elderly but for many years from 1890, the building served refreshments and welcomed visitors to the very popular park. The fountain has altered over the years and much of the more ornate work has disappeared.

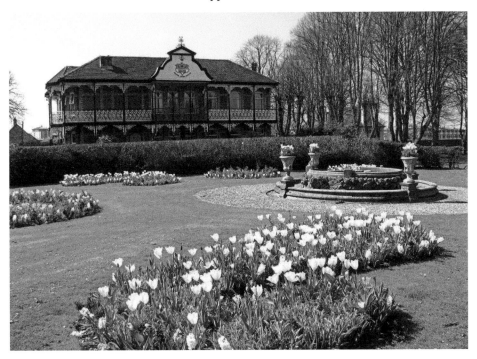

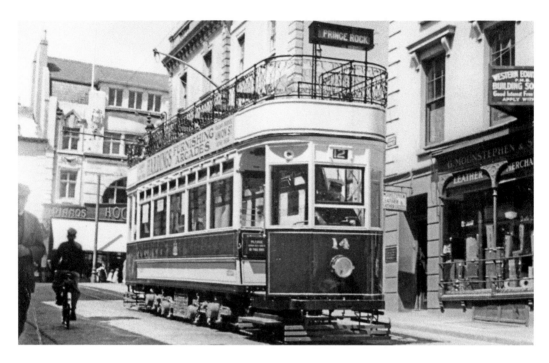

Chapel Street, Devonport

It's hard to imagine nowadays that Chapel Street was once a very busy street with many trams regularly passing by. Chapel Street is still there today but most of the buildings have now disappeared as have the trams. The last tram ran in Plymouth in 1945 and the new photograph shows its more modern replacement.

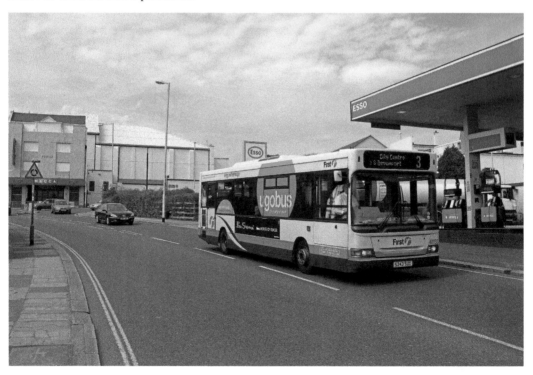

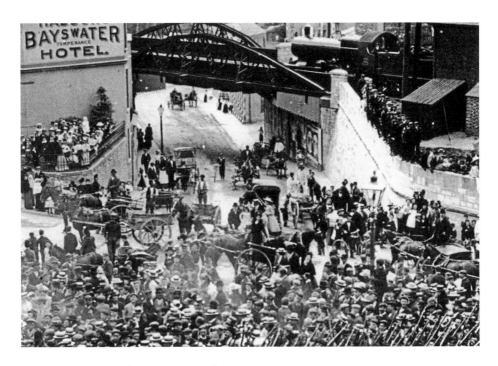

Saltash Road towards Pennycomequick

The first photograph shows a large gathering near the train station at North Hill in the early 1900s. A steam train can be seen crossing the bridge near to Haddon's Bayswater Temperance Hotel. There are many horses and carts on what is now a very busy road full of cars and buses.

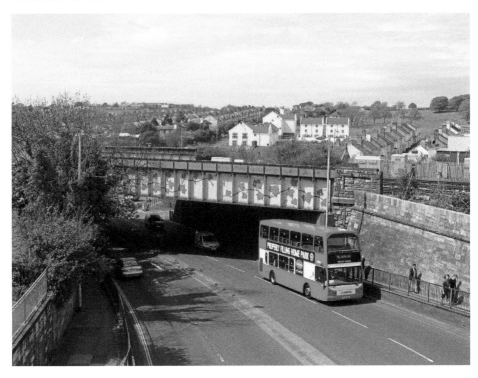

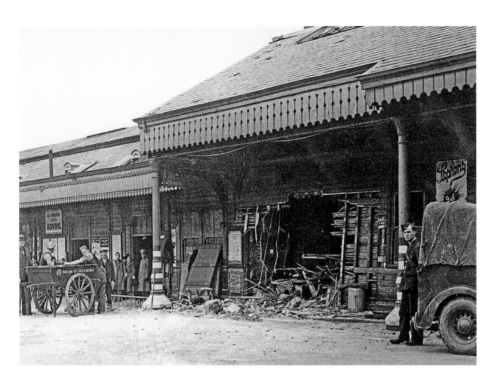

North Road Railway Station

Much has changed over the years since North Road Station was first built in 1877. Rebuilding work to enlarge the station started in 1935 but this was interrupted by the War. The old photograph shows the station after bomb damage and the new photograph shows the station as it appears today.

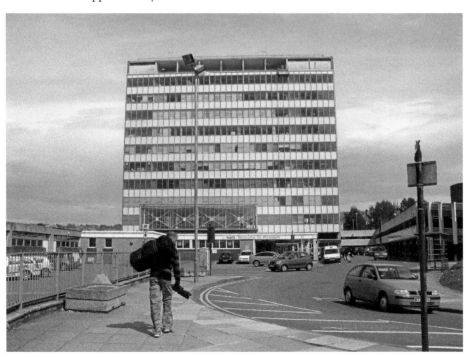

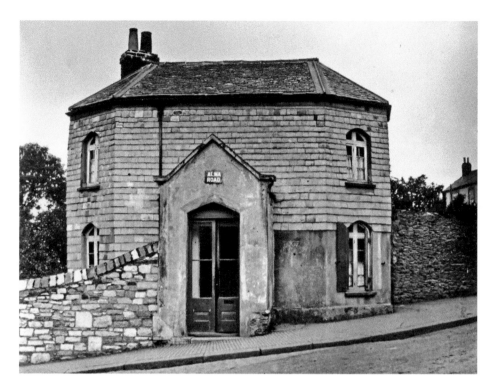

The Toll House, Alma Road, Pennycomequick

The tidal water from Stonehouse Creek once flowed all the way back to Pennycomequick. There was a bridge at this spot and a toll had to be paid to cross it. The original photograph shows the long since disappeared Toll House. When the creek was dammed off in 1890, the area around Pennycomequick soon dried up and there was no need for either the bridge or the Toll House.

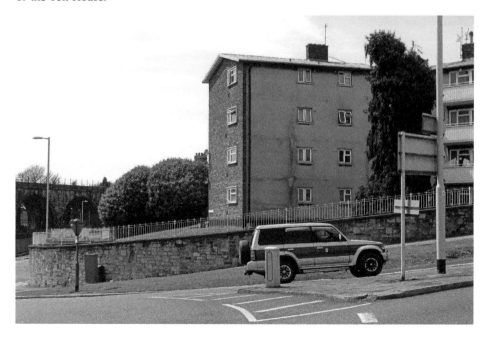

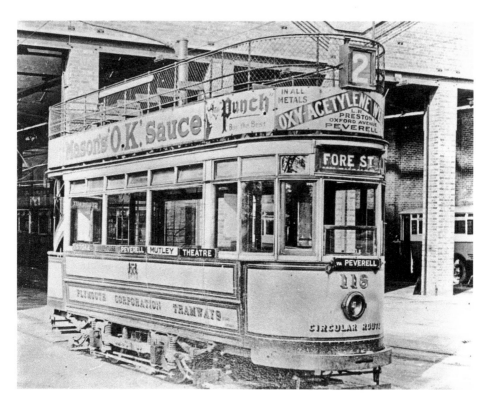

Milehouse Depot

Milehouse Depot has seen many changes over the years. It once housed the many trams that travelled all over Plymouth, Devonport and Stonehouse. The lovely tram shown here is the Number 2 to Fore Street and it's decorated with many local adverts of the day. Today, the depot services the many double and single decker buses that continually pound the roads of Plymouth.

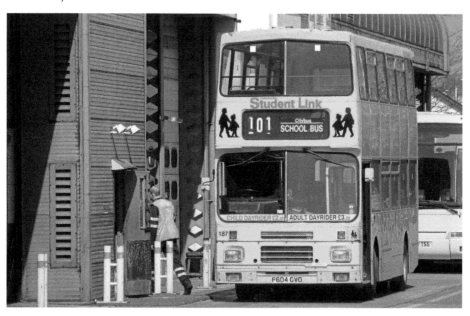

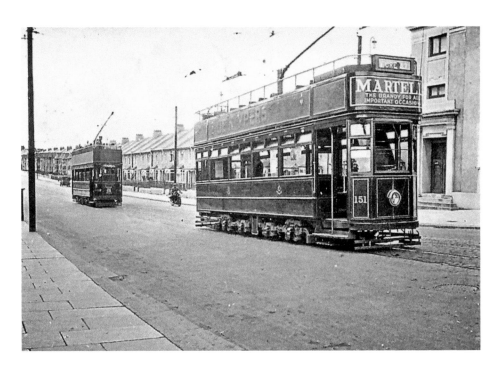

Milehouse Road

The lovely old photograph shows trams travelling along Milehouse Road in the general direction of Central Park. There is only one car and one motorcycle travelling along the road which today is far more busy with traffic of all kinds. The building on the right still remains and today houses the Embassy Snooker Club.

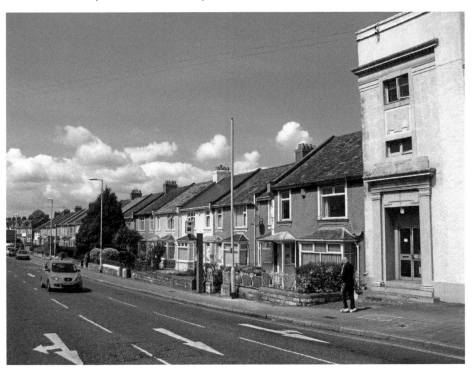

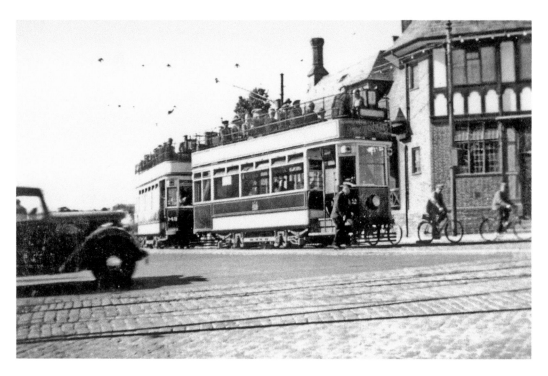

The Britannia, Milehouse

Heavy laden trams pass by the Britannia Inn possibly dropping passengers off at the nearby Plymouth Argyle ground. There are also many cyclists and a car in the first photograph. Today, the trams have long gone but much of the layout of the road and the Britannia Inn remain much the same.

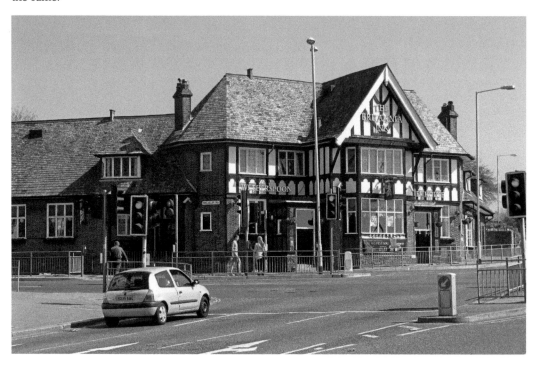

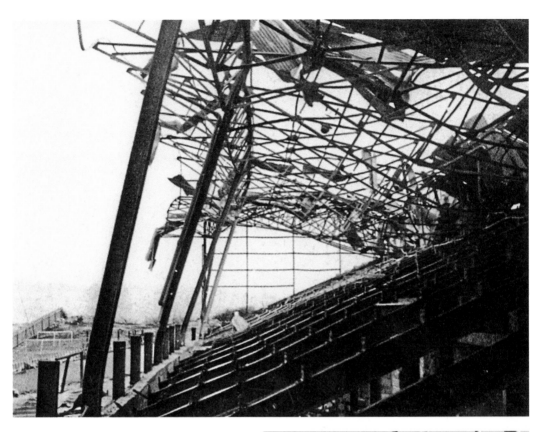

Plymouth Argyle

Home Park has been the home of
Plymouth Argyle since 1901. The ground
at Central Park was bombed during
the War as the first photograph shows.
Rebuilt, the ground reopened in time
for the restart of the Football League
in 1945. Major improvements took
place in 2001 including the complete
redevelopment of the Devonport End,
Lyndhurst Stand and Barn Park End.
There are still plans afoot to improve
the stadium even further and the cost of
this is said to be £50 million.

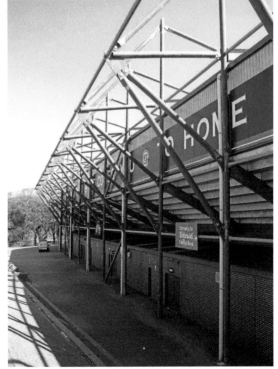

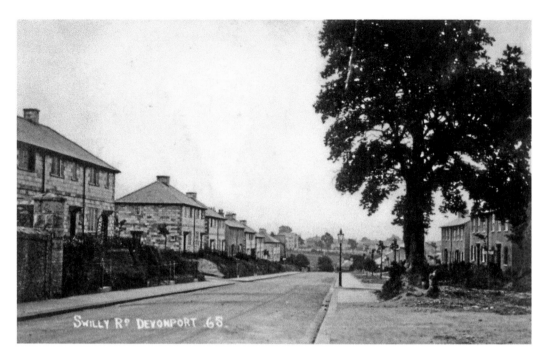

Swilly Road

The houses and layout shown in the first photograph make Swilly Road, now renamed North Prospect Road, easy to recognise. The first photograph shows a street empty of both people and traffic. Following the road downwards eventually leads to Milehouse. In the 1920s, Swilly was the first council housing estate built in Plymouth. It was used to accomodate Officers returning from the First World War. Bombed in the Second World War, the area was later renamed North Prospect in the 1970s.

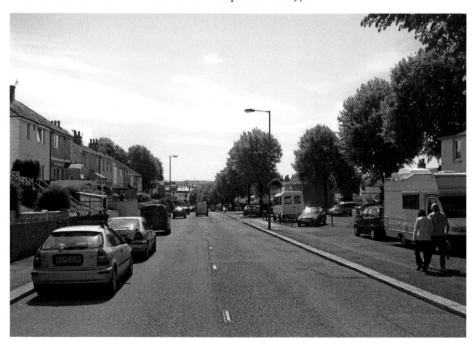

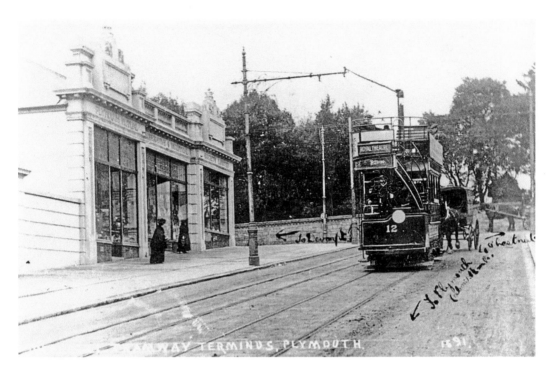

The Co-op, Peverell

The Co-op at Peverell was opened in the early 1900s. The tram in the first photograph has its destination as 'Royal Theatre' which was the termination point by Derry's Clock. The Co-op has greatly expanded over the years and still remains in the same place. The wall at the top of the road is still there and runs along Outland Road.

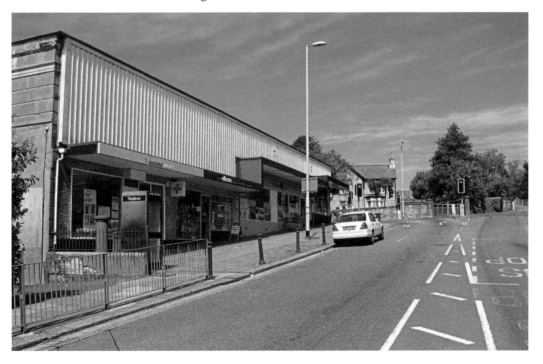

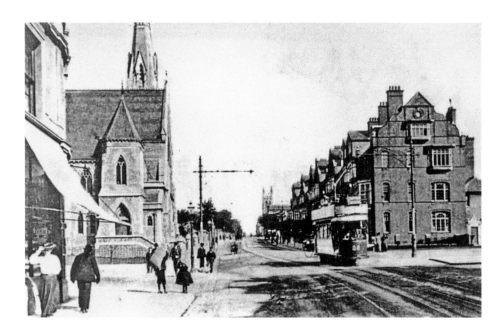

North Hill

Sherwell Church can be seen on the left of the old photograph in about 1905. It was built in 1864. At the time, North Hill was known as Tavistock Road. On 13 January 1941, Sherwell Congregational Chapel was the first of Plymouth's churches to be seriously damaged by enemy bombing. The number 26 tram is on its way to the theatre via Compton. Queen Anne Terrace on the right was once the home of many professionals including doctors. It's now occupied by estate agents and solicitors and, in the later photograph, can be seen under repair.

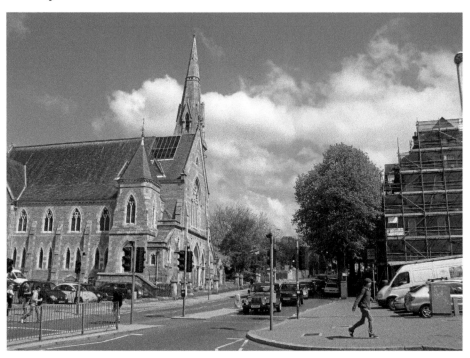

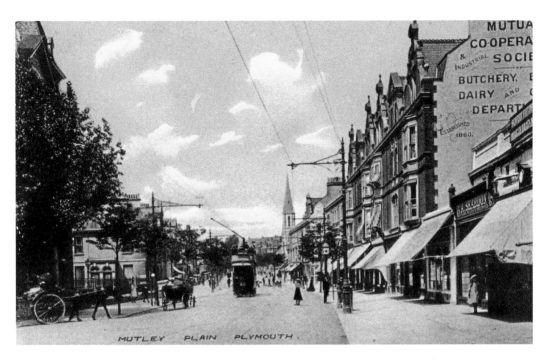

MUTLEY PLAIN PLYMOUTH.

Mutley

Mutley escaped much of the bombing of the Second World War so most of its original buildings still exist. The end wall, painted with the words, 'Mutual Co-operative Society', in the older photograph can clearly be seen in the later photograph, making it easy to work out where this is today. The main changes over the last 100 years include increased traffic, satellite dishes, traffic lights and road signs.

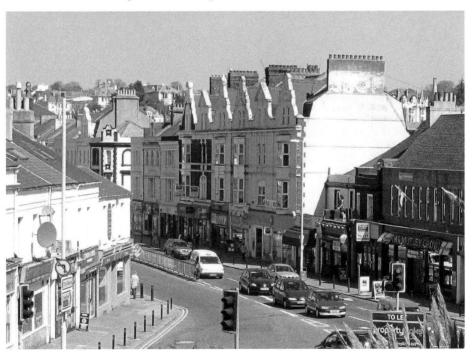

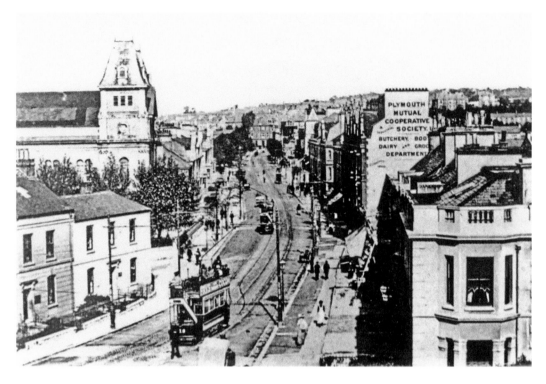

A Tram at Mutley

These two views show the Mutley Baptist Church on the left. Again, the Plymouth Mutual Co-operative Society building can be seen on the right. The later scene gives the appearance of a quiet area but Mutley is usually incredibly full with an endless stream of traffic. The public house on the left is The Junction but it was better known as The Nottingham for many years.

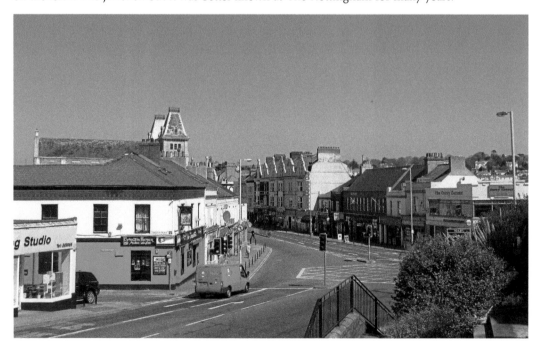

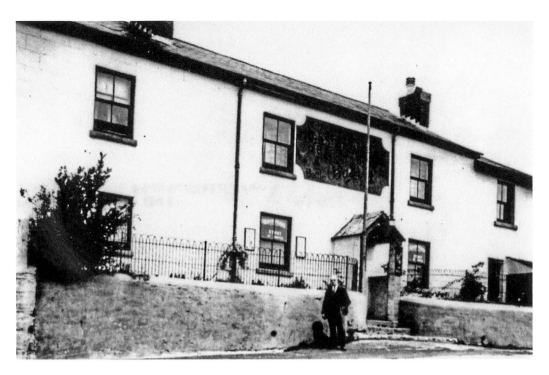

The Blue Monkey Inn, Higher St Budeaux

Although the public house has now been knocked down, the area near to Higher St Budeaux Church will probably always be known as the Blue Monkey. The inn had previously been called Church Inn, St Bude Inn, St Budeaux Inn and Ye Old St Budeaux Inn before becoming the more well-known Blue Monkey.

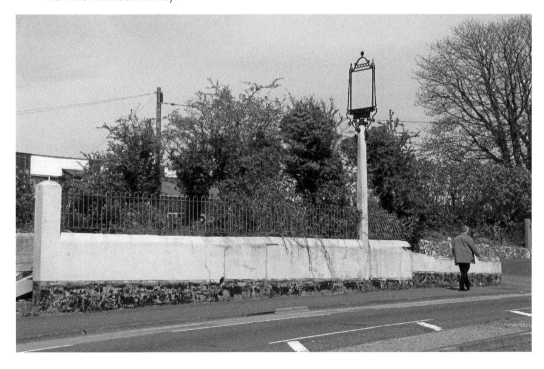

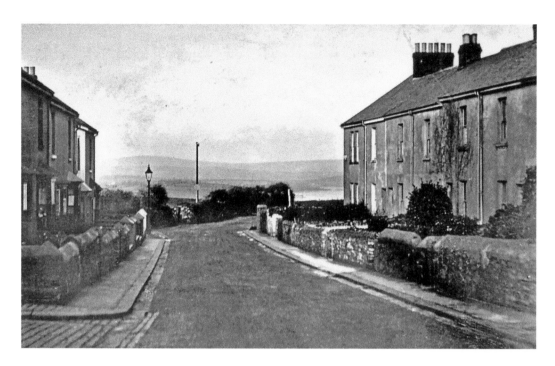

Ernesettle Road

The earlier photograph shows Ernesettle Road in about 1910. These houses still stand today although traffic has increased drastically in the last one hundred years and, in the distance, where you can see just open countryside and the River Tamar, the Parkway now cuts through the land taking travellers to Cornwall over the Tamar Bridge.

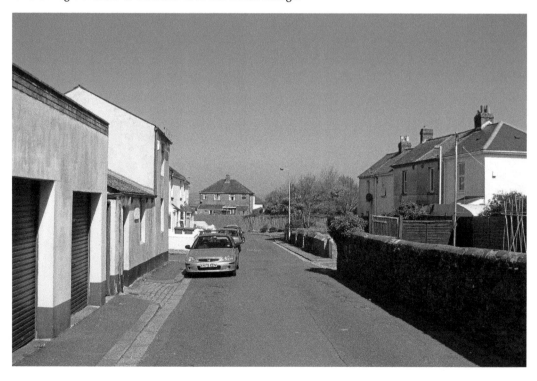

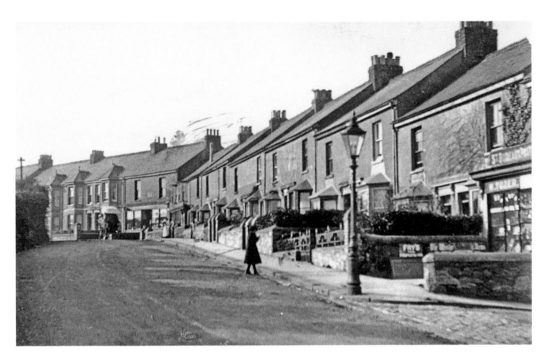

Victoria Road, St Budeaux

This was once Higher Lea Terrace which was located at the top of Higher St Budeaux. The road and the houses have changed little in the last one hundred years. The shop seen on the right was once owned by W. Tozer and was Higher St Budeaux's Post Office.

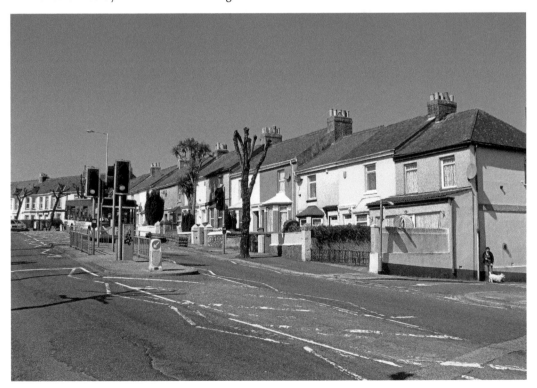

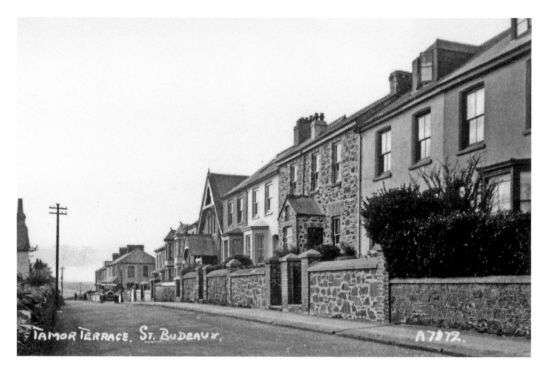

Normandy Way, St Budeaux

Before the Americans passed this way in the Second World War, this street was better known as Tamar Terrace. The houses on the right still remain and the church has been joined to an adjacent house and is now the location of the Royal British Legion Social Club.

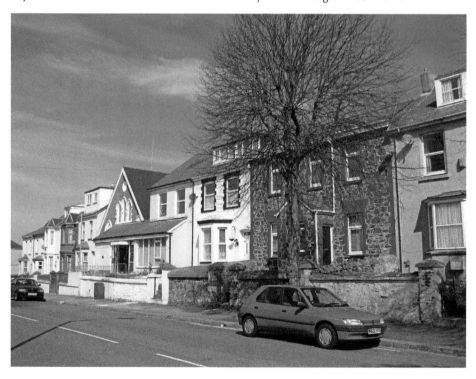

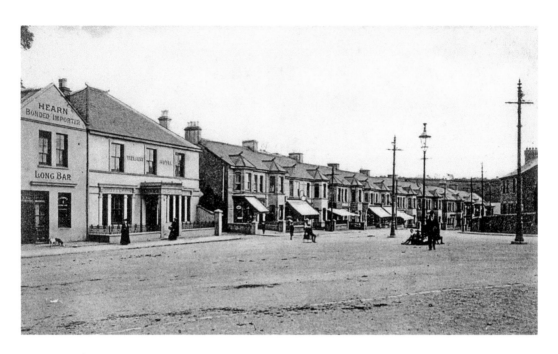

St Budeaux Square

The buildings are all still there, only the road layout and the very busy flow of traffic are different. Today, the Trelawny Inn, painted yellow on the left of the photograph, is empty and has been boarded up after being continually open for over 100 years.

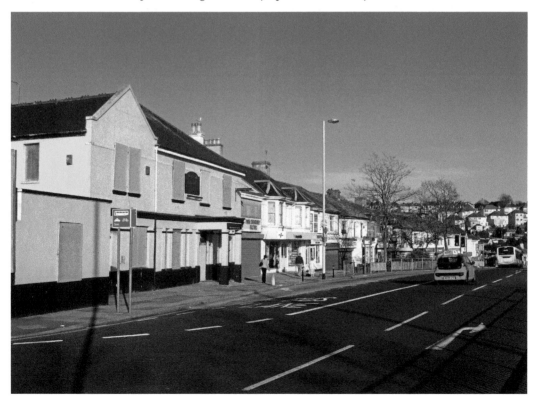

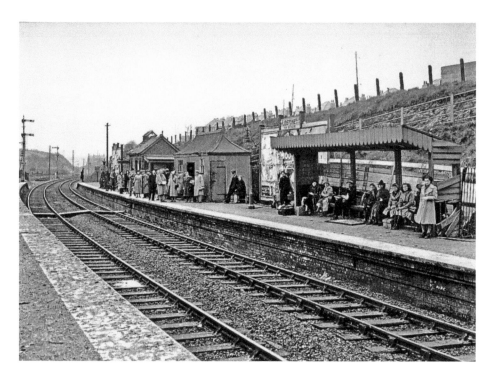

Ferry Road Station, St Budeaux

St Budeaux Station was once very busy taking passengers into Plymouth for work and for shopping. Today, the station is still there but isn't as popular as it once was, with many people having their own cars or catching the bus. The first photograph shows the station after bombing during the Second World war.

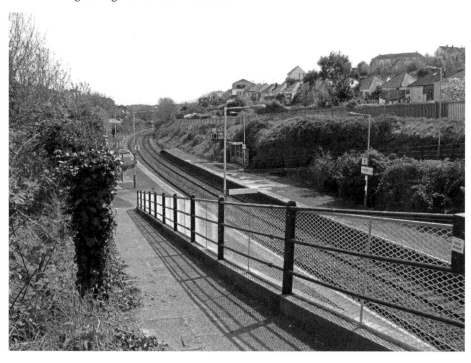

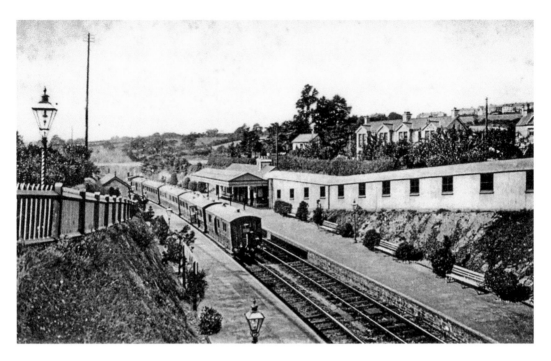

Victoria Road Station, St Budeaux

The covered area on the right of the picture was used to keep dockyard workers dry on rainy days as they waited for their trains into work. It was once a very busy station but today it is eerily quiet and isn't a place that you would want to hang around especially once it starts to get dark.

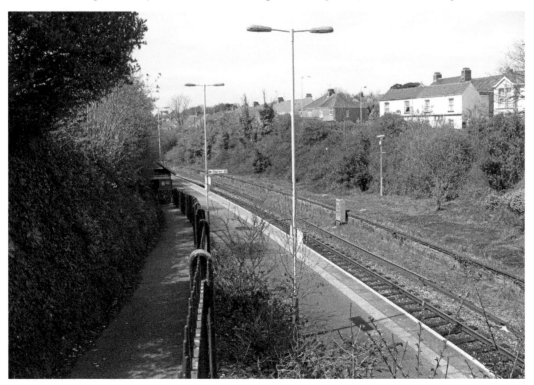

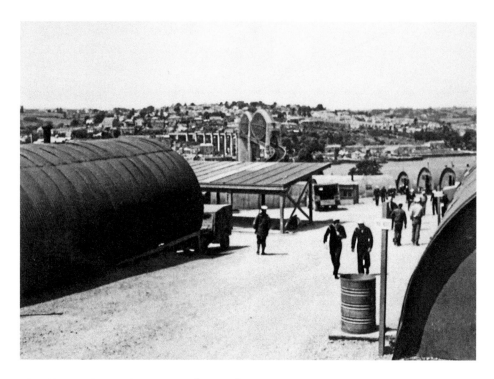

The US Army Base, Vicarage Road, St Budeaux

In January 1944, the US Army set up camp at Vicarage Road in preparation for the D-Day landings. Altogether, it housed 60,000 troops on their way to the Normandy landings. It was also a reception centre for returning troops from July 1944. Vicarage Road was later renamed Normandy Hill and today, much of the area where the camp once was is grassed over.

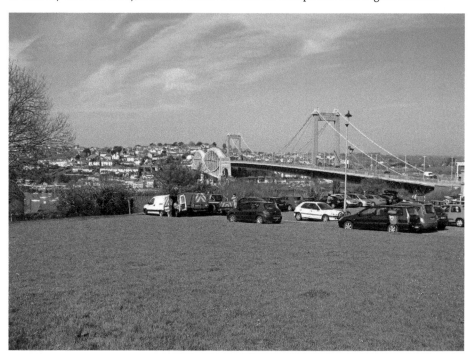

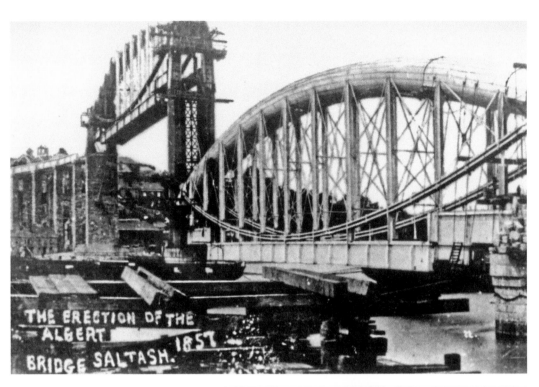

THE ERECTION OF THE ALBERT BRIDGE SALTASH. 1857

The building of the Royal Albert Bridge

The Royal Albert Bridge was built by Isambard Kingdom Brunel and was opened in 1859. The original photograph shows its construction. Today, the Royal Albert Bridge stands beside the Tamar Road Bridge which was opened in 1961. Both bridges are very busy and travelling across the Royal Albert Bridge by train gives a magnificent view of the River Tamar.

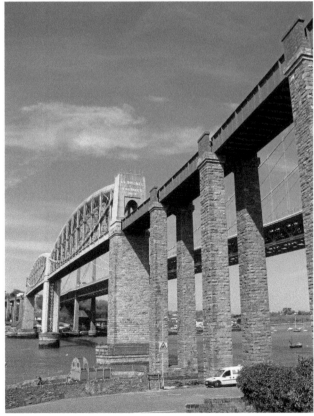

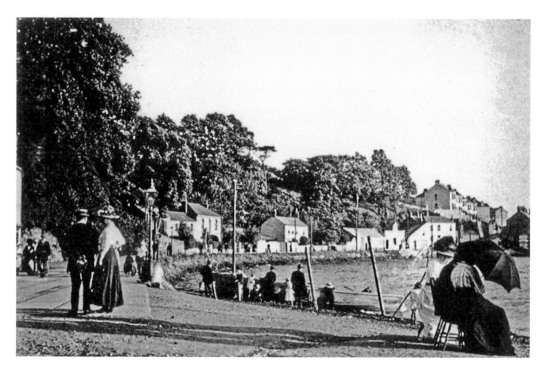

Regatta day, Saltash Passage

The first photograph shows the day before the annual regatta in 1908 featuring many women with fancy hats and parasols. The scene today hasn't really changed that much although a park was built near the waterfront in the 1950s. All of the original houses in the first photograph remain but some have been added to in the last 100 years.

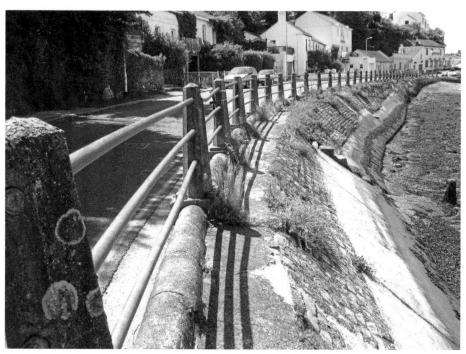

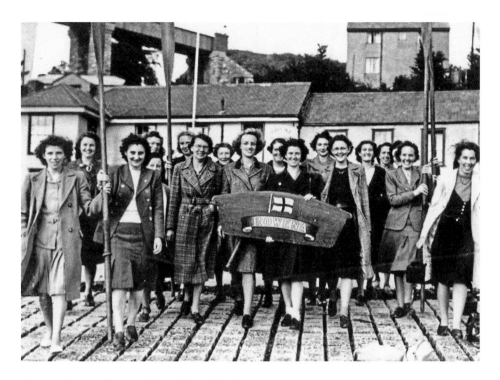

The Baptists Ladies Boating Club, Saltash Passage

The first photograph shows the Baptists Ladies Boating Club holding a board with the name of their boat, *Rowena*. This board was fixed to the transom and used as a backrest in the rear seat. The Royal Albert Bridge Inn is in the background. Some older members of the community might recognise some of the faces in this picture. A solitary house stands on Vicarage Road (later Normandy Hill). This section of the road has long since changed with the inclusion of several newer houses.

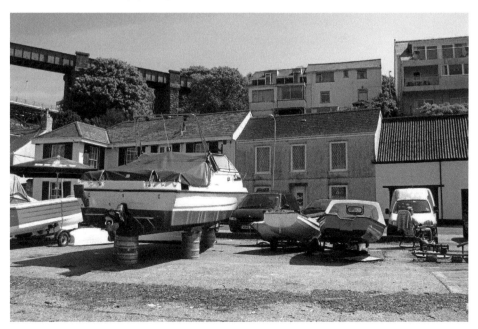

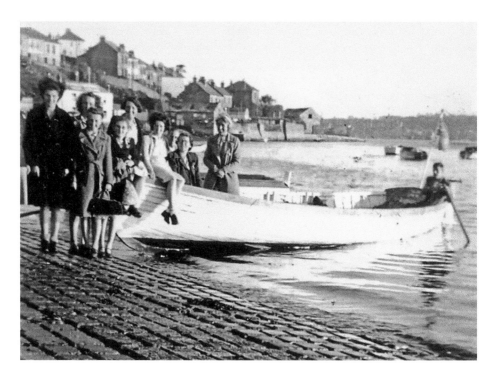

Members of the Boating Club, Saltash Passage

The top photograph shows members of the local Boating Club with their boat at Saltash Passage on 30 June 1947. The 'hards' laid down by the American servicemen in 1944 can be seen in the foreground. The front has now changed a bit and the building on the right of the picture has now gone and has been replaced by the yacht club. The area will be instantly recognisable to most residents of St Budeaux and the houses in the background have changed little over the years.

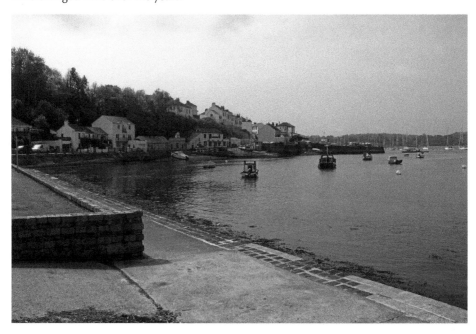

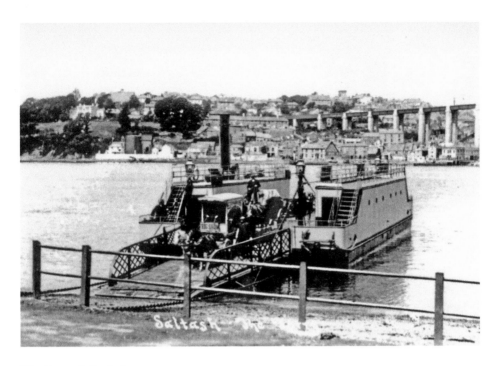

The Ferry, Saltash Passage

The ferry ran for hundreds of years before being discontinued in 1961 when the Tamar Bridge was opened to road traffic. The view hasn't changed too much and the slipway can still be seen, as can the slipway on the Saltash side. Many of the older buildings on the Saltash side have long since been demolished.

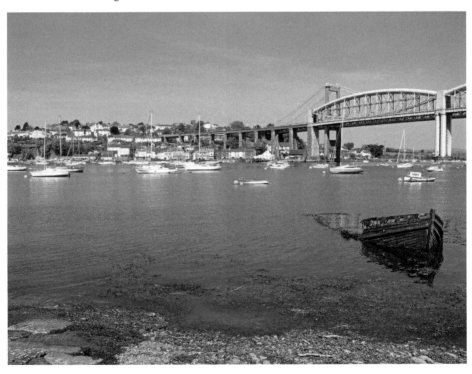

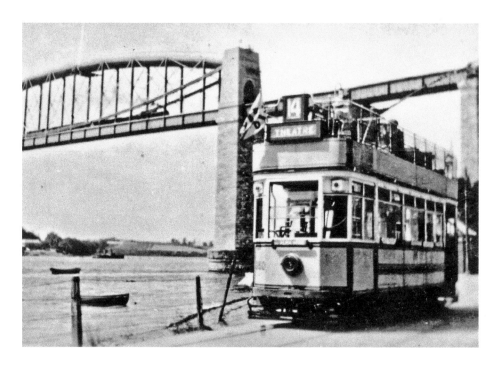

A Tram, Saltash Passage

It's been a long time since trams ran to Saltash Passage. Today, the area hasn't even got a bus service. The journey from the centre of Plymouth to Saltash Passage was the longest tram journey you could take back then, covering about 9 miles. Although, the trams are long gone, the tramlines still lie beneath the modern tarmac road and occasionally appear whenever there's a pothole or other roadworks.

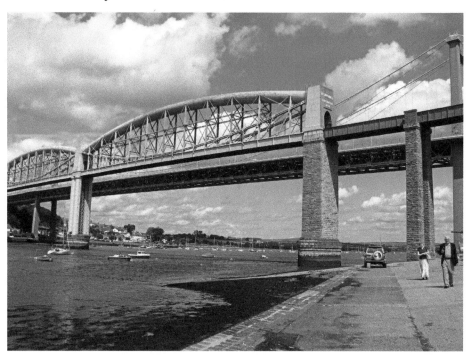

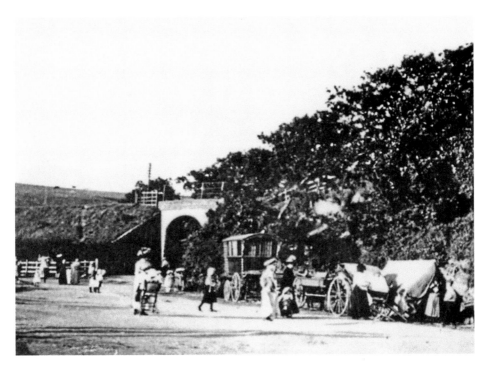

Gypsies, Saltash Passage

In the early 1900s, gypsies lived beside the Royal Albert Bridge and made and sold pegs. It was said that they lived on a diet of baked hedgehogs. Today, the area seen in the first photograph, falls within MOD property and leads to the nearby armaments depot on the River Tamar.

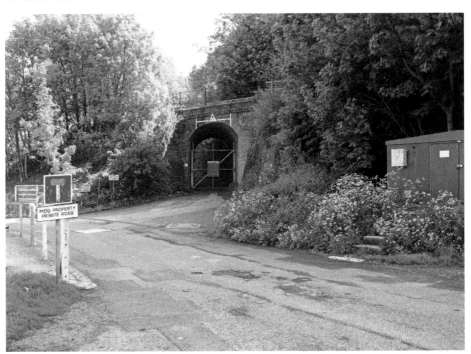

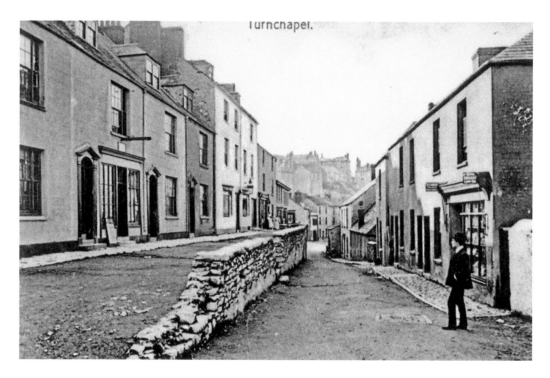

Turnchapel

Parts of Turnchapel have changed little over the years as can be seen in these two photographs. Funnily enough, a 'Victorian' lamppost appears in the later photograph but was never there in the original. Modern wheelie bins can be seen chained to the nearby fence but overall, the scene remains much the same.

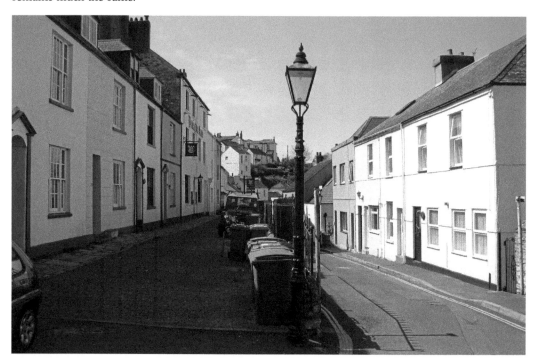